D0207970

The Nigerian Americans

Nigeria. Courtesy of Bookcomp.

The Nigerian Americans

Kalu Ogbaa

THE NEW AMERICANS

Ronald H. Bayor, Series Editor

GREENWOOD PRESS

Westport, Connecticut • London

Library of Congress Cataloging-in-Publication Data

Ogbaa, Kalu
  The Nigerian Americans / Kalu Ogbaa.
    p.   cm.—(The New Americans, ISSN 1092–6364)
  Includes bibliographical references (p.   ) and index.
  ISBN 0–313–31964–2 (alk. paper)
  1. Nigerian Americans. 2. Immigrants—United States. 3. Nigerian Americans—Social
  conditions. I. Title. II. New Americans (Westport, Conn.)
E184.N55O36   2003
305.896'69073—dc21   2003040840

British Library Cataloguing in Publication Data is available.

Library of Congress Catalog Card Number: 2003040840
ISBN: 0–313–31964–2
ISSN: 1092–6364

First published in 2003

Greenwood Press, 88 Post Road West, Westport, CT 06881
An imprint of Greenwood Publishing Group, Inc.
www.greenwood.com

Printed in the United States of America

The paper used in this book complies with the
Permanent Paper Standard issued by the National
Information Standards Organization (Z39.48–1984).

10   9   8   7   6   5   4   3   2   1

To Uchenna, Adanne, Ekeoma, and Steve
with love and best wishes
Umu m, uwa dikwara unu nile mma;
o bu nna unu nagozi unu

Contents

Series Foreword

Oscar Handlin, a prominent historian, once wrote, "I thought to write a history of the immigrants in America. Then I discovered that the immigrants were American history." The United States has always been a nation of nations where people from every region of the world have come to begin a new life. Other countries such as Canada, Argentina, and Australia also have had substantial immigration, but the United States is still unique in the diversity of nationalities and the great numbers of migrating people who have come to its shores.

Who are these immigrants? Why did they decide to come? How well have they adjusted to this new land? What has been the reaction to them? These are some of the questions the books in this "The New Americans" series seek to answer. There have been many studies about earlier waves of immigrants—e.g., the English, Irish, Germans, Jews, Italians, and Poles—but relatively little has been written about the newer groups—those arriving in the last thirty years, since the passage of a new immigration law in 1965. This series is designed to correct that situation and to introduce these groups to the rest of America.

Each book in this series discusses one of these groups, and each is written by an expert on those immigrants. The volumes cover the new migration from primarily Asia, Latin America, and the Caribbean, including the Koreans, Cambodians, Filipinos, Vietnamese, South Asians such as Indians and Pakistanis, Chinese from both China and Taiwan, Haitians, Jamaicans, Cubans, Dominicans, Mexicans, Puerto Ricans (even though they are already U.S. citizens), and Jews from the former Soviet Union. Although some of these people, such as Jews, have been in America since colonial times, this series concentrates on their recent migrations, and thereby offers its unique contribution.

These volumes are designed for high school and general readers who want to learn more about their new neighbors. Each author has provided information about the land of origin, its history and culture, the reasons for migrating, and the ethnic culture as it began to adjust to American life. Readers will find fascinating details on religion, politics, foods, festivals, gender roles, employment trends, and general community life. They will learn how Vietnamese immigrants differ from Cuban immigrants and, yet, how they are also alike in many ways. Each book is arranged to offer an in-depth look at the particular immigrant group but also to enable readers to compare one group with another. The volumes also contain brief biographical profiles of notable individuals, tables noting each group's immigration, and a short bibliography of readily available books and articles for further reading. Most contain a glossary of foreign words and phrases.

Students and others who read these volumes will secure a better understanding of the age-old questions of "who is an American" and "how does the assimilation process work?" Similar to their nineteenth- and early twentieth-century forebears, many Americans today doubt the value of immigration and fear the influx of individuals who look and sound different from those who had come earlier. If comparable books had been written one hundred years ago, they would have done much to help dispel readers' unwarranted fears of the newcomers. Nobody today would question, for example, the role of those of Irish or Italian ancestry as Americans; yet, this was a serious issue in our history and a source of great conflict. It is time to look at our recent arrivals, to understand their history and culture, their skills, their place in the United States, and their hopes and dreams as Americans.

The United States is a vastly different country than it was at the beginning of the twentieth century. The economy has shifted away from industrial jobs; the civil rights movement has changed minority-majority relations and, along with the women's movement, brought more people into the economic mainstream. Yet one aspect of American life remains strikingly similar—we are still the world's main immigrant-receiving nation and, as in every period of American history, we are still a nation of immigrants. It is essential that we attempt to learn about and understand this long-term process of migration and assimilation.

Ronald H. Bayor
Georgia Institute of Technology

Acknowledgments

I wish to express my heart-felt gratitude to Professor J. Philip Smith, for providing a private grant that enabled me financially to embark on the research project, and for his encouragement and support for my overall scholarship and research activities at Southern Connecticut State University; to Professor Ellen Beatty of the faculty development unit of the Office of the Vice President for Academic Affairs at Southern Connecticut State University, for providing secretarial support; to Professor Ronald H. Bayor, series editor of Greenwood Press's "The New Americans" series, for allowing me to participate in the project; to the Nigerian Americans who permitted me to use their profiles, which appear in the appendix; and, above all, to my children, whose future lives in America have been the major cause of my writing about Africa, Nigeria, and the Igbo in this study and in other studies I have published in the recent past. For all their kind help, I am very grateful.

PART I
BACKGROUND

1

Nigerian American Ethnic Roots: The Land, History, People, and Culture

Nigerian Americans, as well as other immigrants from sub-Saharan African countries, are generally regarded by other Americans as either foreigners in this land of immigrants or appendages to the African American population. However, beginning from the mid-1970s, Nigerians have sought from their fellow Americans the kind of recognition and respect accorded to other new immigrant groups from Asia, Eastern Europe, Latin America, and the Caribbean. They believe they deserve equal acknowledgment because of the important contributions they have been making to all aspects of their new nation, which many Americans are not aware of. That lack of awareness of the new immigrants' contributions to the United States may have prompted President John F. Kennedy to acknowledge publicly that "the contribution of immigrants can be seen in every aspect of our national life. We see it in religion, in politics, in business, in the arts, in education, even in athletics and in entertainment. There is no part of our nation that has not been touched by our immigrant background" (Kennedy 1964, 3). The understanding of Nigerian Americans and their contributions to our national life begins with an examination of their ethnic background—the land of Nigeria and its history, people, and culture—which informs and influences their lives as immigrants in the United States.

LAND

Nigeria, one of the biggest countries in Africa, is situated on the eastern end of the West African region: it lies east of the Republic of Benin, south of the Republic of Niger and the Republic of Chad, west of the Republic of Cameroon, and north of the Bight of Benin and Bight of Biafra in the Atlantic Ocean's Gulf of Guinea. It occupies an area of approximately 923,768.64 square kilometers (577,355.40 square miles) (Consulate General of Nigeria, interview by author, New York, June 12, 2001). In comparative terms, Nigeria is larger than the states of California, Nevada, and Utah combined. Its area is about the same as that occupied collectively by the states of North Dakota, South Dakota, Minnesota, Iowa, and Nebraska and slightly less than the combined areas of Ireland, the United Kingdom and Northern Ireland, France, Belgium, and the Netherlands. At its widest east-west span, it stretches about 767 kilometers (479.375 miles), and from north to south, about 1,605 kilometers (1,003.125 miles).

Because the country is situated between latitudes 4° and 14° north of the Equator and longitudes 3° and 14° east, its climate varies from tropical in the south to semitropical in the central region, and semi-arid to arid in the far north. There are two distinct seasons in the year, although each is experienced to be of different length and intensity, depending on location. "The dry season, generally November–March, is characterized by the Harmattan, a dry wind laden with fine dust particles originating from the Sahara Desert in the North, and blowing in a south-westerly direction across the West African region. In the rainy season, April–October, the direction of the wind reverses, and the moisture-laden south-west trade winds blow on-shore and towards the interior, bringing heavy rains to most of the country" (Bell-Gam and Iyam 1985, xvii).

Usually, temperatures remain high throughout the year in most parts of the country, with little seasonal variation. The distance from the ocean and elevation dictate the climate. Because the whole country is situated within the tropics (as noted previously), the temperature is usually warm.

The major rivers that affect the climatic and economic conditions of the country are the Niger, Benue, Sokoto, Kaduna, Anambra, Katsina-Ala, Delta, Bonny, Cross, and Qua Iboe. Added to these rivers is a lake with an area of 1,236 square kilometers (772.50 square miles), which was created on the River Niger by the construction of the Kainji hydroelectric dam, about 112 kilometers (70 miles) north of Jebba. The dam, which is also used to control the flow of the Niger flood waters, has since made the river navigable throughout the year from Escravos to Niamey in the Niger Republic, a distance of more than 1,600 kilometers (1,000 miles) (Consulate General of Nigeria, interview by author, New York, June 12, 2001).

HISTORY

The formal creation of Nigeria as a country began in the year 1900, when the West African territories around River Niger and River Benue were acquired by Great Britain as northern and southern protectorates, following the scramble for and partition of Africa by various European countries. By 1914, the protectorates were amalgamated to form one British colonial country by Sir Frederick Lugard, its first governor-general, who named it Nigeria after the great river, Niger, that transverses the country from north to south.

Before those two historic dates, however, Nigeria had had a long and checkered history that goes as far back as 400 B.C. That history was derived in part from the people's oral tales, because they had an oral culture, and more authoritatively from archaeological artifacts excavated by British archaeologists, anthropologists, and historians, who worked for the British university college at Ibadan in Nigeria and for the British administration, which needed a lot of information on the colonial peoples that would help it to govern well and to sustain British colonialism and empire in that part of Africa.

One of the renowned professors at Ibadan, Thurston Shaw, who did a lot of archaeological work in Nigeria, especially at Igbo-Ukwu in Igboland, asserts that the Nigerian prehistory and cultural developments are traceable to the divisions in the West African Iron Age:

1. The Early Contact Period: c. 400 B.C.–A.D. 700
2. Northern Contact Period: c. A.D. 700–A.D. 1475
3. Southern Contact Period: c. A.D. 1475–A.D. 1850
4. Inland Contact Period: after A.D. 1850. (Shaw 1980, 35–36)

Events of these historical periods help to explain not only the evolutionary growth of the country but also the sociocultural and geopolitical differences in Nigeria from the prehistorical times through the present time.

During the early contact period, Nigeria was a closed society. It had limited contact with the outside world, including the nomadic Arabs who traveled through the area in search of gold. Instead, Nigerian peoples were busy developing their agricultural systems and skills in manufacturing iron and earthen wares for personal use and trade by barter with their neighbors. At Taruga, about 35 kilometers (21.875 miles) south of Abuja (the present-day capital of Nigeria), a number of iron-smelting furnaces have been excavated that have produced radiocarbon dates from the fifth to the third centuries B.C. Excavations in occupation mounds, carried out as part of the rescue archaeology conducted in the area now flooded by the Kainji Dam on the river Niger, indicated the presence of iron in this area by the second century B.C.

Furthermore, the iron-smelting sites of Taruga were associated with terracotta figurines of the distinctive artistic style named after the Nigerian village of Nok, where they were first found. Nok culture was first known as a result of the recovery of archaeological remains from the tin-bearing gravels west of the Jos Plateau in the course of mining operations. These remains consisted of ground stone axes and smaller stone tools, iron axes and other iron tools, the baked clay draught pipe used in iron smelting, quartz lip-plugs and other ornaments, and, above all, the striking terra-cotta. Down south, the most spectacular archaeological find is the Igbo-Ukwu Bronze Altar, with solid panels decorated with conventionalized spiders overlaying a geometric pattern, which evidences the best in prehistoric Igbo art and technology.

Igbo prehistory has also been revealed in archaeological excavations. The Igbo people probably first lived at the Cross River and the Anambra Valley-Nsukka escapement (Isichei 1976, 3–4). In each of these areas, late Stone Age sites have been excavated. A rock shelter at Afikpo was first inhabited about five thousand years ago by people who made rough red pottery and a variety of stone tools—hoes, knives, pounders, and so on. In the town of Ibagwa in the Nsukka area, a rock shelter has yielded stone tools and pottery. Some of the pottery from these excavations is 4,500 years old.

Such archaeological artifacts have been excavated as well from Yorubaland in the southwest, Daima in Borno State, and Kanuri in the Yobe valley. All these go to prove that precolonial Nigeria had a rich artistic culture and technological know-how that sustained the people before the coming of the whites into the country.

The northern contact period in Nigerian history is a time when long-distance trade, however indirect, began to play an increasingly important role in influencing not only economic but social and political patterns. Trade brought wealth to certain parts of West Africa, and that helped to provide the basis for social stratification and state formations. According to Shaw, "Now also we are no longer entirely dependent on archaeological information but begin in addition to get Arab historical records" (1980, 41). During this period, Arabs from North Africa had started trade businesses with ancient Ghana, the land of gold, which was so militarily and financially powerful that it played the role of a middleman between gold-producing West Africa (including parts of Nigeria) and the Islamic world. Ghana was succeeded by Mali, the ancient West Sudan, which not only had wealth but had built the first organized university in Timbuktu—a fact that many in the Western world have been reluctant to acknowledge, either because the university was founded in a black country or because its curriculum was Islamic.

Going eastward from Mali, the Arabs on the gold route came in contact with northern Nigerian cites such as Katsina, Kano, Kanuri, and Zaria, where they established trade links and Islamic religion. But they did not go to the southern ends of the country because of the natural geographic and climatic divide, which did not promote any commercial or cultural interaction between the north and the south. Consequently, 90 percent of Nigerian Muslims live in the north and 80 percent of the Christians live in the south, and that has been a perennial source of discord in the sociocultural, economic, educational, political, and religious institutions of the nation.

The southern contact period is characterized by the coming of European voyagers to the coastal territories of Nigeria, such as Lagos, Bonny, Port Harcourt, Warri, Calabar, and Itu, some of which have since developed into the modern Nigerian states of Lagos, Delta, Bayelsa, Rivers, Akwa Ibom, and Cross River, all in southern Nigeria. According to Shaw, at the beginning of this period, northern contacts remained much more important, and it was the period when the Songhai empire took over from Mali the role of middleman between West Africa and the Islamic world (1980, 52).

The most important event with global significance that took place in Nigeria during this period is the human slave trade. Portuguese voyagers visited some coastal towns of West Africa, especially those in Senegal and Gambia as well as those in Nigeria (mentioned previously), during the mid-1400s. In fact, from 1450–92, the Portuguese engaged Nigeria in trade by barter. However, in search of a supply of labor for the Spanish colonies in the New World, from 1492 through the Industrial Revolution of the 1830s, the Portuguese raided those West African coasts for slaves, and their action encouraged other European nations to engage in the purchase and use of Africans as slaves in the New World. For example, Britain alone shipped away 135,000 slaves per year from Africa on the average, and from that yearly figure, 13,000 came from Nigeria. This is how the African American ancestors were forced to come here; this is how continental Africa was depopulated.

Furthermore, by 1494, some European countries began scrambling for African slaves and later for some industrial raw materials to sustain the European Industrial Revolution. As a result of the envy, enmity, and greed that the competitive scramble provoked, a meeting of the European nations was called in December 1884 in which they formally partitioned Africa in January 1885, and Nigeria was officially given to Great Britain to colonize. In 1840, European missionaries were already working in southern Nigeria. Their activities in Nigeria led to the establishment of Christianity and churches, mission schools and Western education, as well as European culture. Thus, while the British government agents began to colonize the Nigerian territories, the missionaries and teachers colonized the minds of the young Nigerians whom they taught. That way Nigeria began to lose its sovereignty gradually but surely.

The inland contact period is when the British colonization process was completed, and the people witnessed a total loss of their sovereignty to

Britain. After 1885, the national borders of Nigeria, its politics and governance, a national language, and educational policies were all clearly defined and protected against attacks by internal and external enemies of the British colonizers. With the colonization of the country came the opening up of Nigeria, once a closed society, to the outside world for commerce but only under British terms. Also, the society gradually transformed from being an oral culture into a literate nation. Because of that, the historical documents, both oral and written, became more and more plentiful, and only occasionally did archaeological method have much to contribute to the story of Nigeria. The country continued to be governed by the British until October 1, 1960, when Nigeria won its political independence. Three years later, it became the Federal Republic of Nigeria.

The postcolonial history is a sorry one; it is one that is full of rhythms of violence and profuse bloodbaths. Barely three years after Nigeria attained republican status, the quiet optimism that its citizens enjoyed died down as a result of the new political, social, and economic problems. Nigeria was in danger of disintegration. On the political front, two of the four regions of the country were unstable: Western Region had bloody political crises, as did the Tiv area of Northern Region. Both areas revolted openly against their local governments. As a result, both regions produced political turmoil that threatened the unity of the entire nation. In fact, the ethnic antagonism and prejudice, which the British had managed to suppress during the colonial days, resurfaced. It led to general corruption and nepotism at all levels of government and society, including the military, judiciary, police, civil service, and universities.

Furthermore, Western education had stratified and polarized people and bred social and economic warfare between city and village dwellers, the educated and the uneducated, the ruling class (politicians) and the ruled (citizens), and the rich and the poor. Thus, there was general discontent throughout the country. In the end, a cloud of uncertainty hung over the nation. Nothing seemed to work, in spite of the peaceful demonstrations by students and labor unions against the regional and federal governments. Finally, on January 15, 1966, the army staged a bloody coup that overthrew the federal government and ushered in a military regime. It was generally believed that the leaders of the coup planners were Igbo. Unfortunately, that same day, assassinations occurred in Kaduna (Hausa area and capital of Northern Region), and at Ibadan (Yoruba area and capital of Western Region). None occurred in Benin (capital of Midwest Region, whose premier was Igbo), or in Enugu (Igbo area and capital of Eastern Region). The coup planners handed over the governance of the nation to the highest-ranking

Nigerian military officer, Major-General Johnson T. U. Aguiyi-Ironsi, an Igbo. He had been the first African Force Commander of the United Nations Peace-Keeping Operation during the Congo Crisis, 1960–63.

During his brief administration, Aguiyi-Ironsi took steps to unite the country by abolishing (through a decree) the regional government system that had promoted separatism and mistrust. In its place, he introduced a unitary government that saw the entire country as one territory. Unfortunately, Northerners, whose political leaders had been assassinated during the January 15, 1966, coup, misinterpreted his intentions. They feared that the unitary government was a plot by Igbo leaders to dominate the country. In a second military coup, which was led by Northern military leaders, Aguiyi-Ironsi and a number of high-ranking Igbo officers were assassinated.

When news of the second coup, which took place on July 29, 1966, spread, Northern military officers, the police, and armed civilians of Hausa and Fulani peoples went on a rampage, killing every Igbo they could find in northern cities such as Kano and Kaduna to avenge the deaths of those killed in the first coup. The massacre reached the proportion of an ethnic cleansing, a kind of pogrom. Resultantly, the military governor of Eastern Nigeria, Colonel Chukwuemeka Odumegwu-Ojukwu, asked all Easterners living in the North to return to the East. They all abandoned their businesses and jobs and returned to the safety of their homeland.

With Aguiyi-Ironsi gone, Easterners' fear was heightened by the emergence of Colonel Yakubu Gowon, a Hausa, as the new head of state and commander-in-chief of the armed forces of Nigeria. He reinstated the regional government system that General Aguiyi-Ironsi had abolished in spite of its weaknesses. In the end, when Colonel Odumegwu-Ojukwu sought and failed to see a peaceful resolution of the military impasse that affected his region more than any other parts of the country, he and his consultative assembly (an informal congress of elders) met in Enugu to declare the region a sovereign state. Colonel Odumegwu-Ojukwu declared the seceding Eastern Nigeria the Republic of Biafra on May 27, 1967.

Colonel Gowon reacted to the secession with what he called "police action" against the region (which later became a full-blown war), with which he intended to unite the country. The Nigeria-Biafra War was fought from July 1967 through January 15, 1970, when the Biafrans surrendered to the federal troops in order to stop the bloodbath that had claimed 1.5 million lives of the Igbo people (Ogbaa 1995, 43–49).

From 1970 through 1999, Nigeria was ruled by various Hausa/Fulani-led military regimes that ousted one another through bloody coups and counter-coups. Except for a brief civilian interregnum of the Shagari administration from 1979 to 1982, from 1960 (when Nigeria became politically independent of Britain) until 1999, Nigeria was under military rule. Abuse of fundamental human rights, hunger and disease, corruption and graft, and political debauchery, as well as economic and social deprivations characterized the military regimes and drove many Nigerians to seek refuge outside the country. At last, a little ray of hope came when the United States, under the Clinton administration, helped Nigeria to experiment once more with democratic governance beginning in May 1999 under the Olusegun Obasanjo administration. Since then, politicians have been taking positive steps to bring back Nigeria to the course of democracy. They may not have totally succeeded in that effort, but at least they are facing the right direction toward achieving democracy.

Its ugly history notwithstanding, Nigeria has always attracted visitors from the outside world because of its human and natural resources, as well as its economic potentialities. For instance, a greater proportion of the African slaves, who supplied forced, free labor to Europe and the Americas, came from Nigeria. Its agricultural products, such as hardwood timber, cocoa, coffee, and palm oil and kernel, and mineral wealth, such as columbite, iron ore, tin, lignite, copper, limestone, lead, and coal, sustained the British and other European factories during and after the Industrial Revolution. In modern times, Nigeria has supplied crude oil for the manufacture of gasoline and other petroleum products to the industrialized world, especially the United States, which depended to a very large extent on oil from Nigeria during the 1967 and 1973 Arab-Israeli wars. Nigeria continues to play a vital role as an oil supplier to the world, as it is an important member of the oil cartel OPEC (Organization of Petroleum Exporting Countries).

PEOPLE

In the year 2001, the population of Nigeria was 126,635,626. That makes Nigeria the most populous country in Africa, and by some estimates, it has the tenth-largest population in the world. Also, Nigeria is a multi-ethnic nation inhabited by about 440 ethnic groups. However, three of those ethnic groups account for 66 percent of the total population: the Hausa, who live mainly in the north; the Igbo, who live in the southeast; and the Yoruba, who live in the southwest. Ethnic minority groups that have relatively small populations include the Edo, Efik/Ibibio, Ekoi, and Ijaw, who live in the south, and the Fulani, Kanuri, Nupe, Chamba, and Tiv in the north. Other ethnic groups are quite small.

All the Nigerian ethnic groups are black. For that reason, race is not an issue in Nigeria as it is in the United States, but ethnicity is. Analogous to racial discrimination and deprivation in the United States, Nigeria's problems emanate from ethnic domination and marginilization, which some people call *tribalism*. The sources of all the major sociopolitical, religious, and economic upheavals in Nigeria, including the 1967–70 civil war, can be traced back to the struggle for power between the three dominant ethnic groups.

In fairness to the majority groups, however, it should be noted that they were also in the front lines of the battle to prevent the British from creating and colonizing the country in the first place. Even though they failed in that effort and Britain prevailed, the three groups produced such savvy political leaders as Dr. Nnamdi Azikiwe (an Igbo), Chief Obafemi Awolowo (a Yoruba), and Sir Abubakar Tafawa Balewa (a Hausa/Fulani), who fought politically to free Nigeria from colonization. This time the Nigerians prevailed over the British, and all Nigerian peoples became free at last.

The Igbo people appeared to dominate other ethnic groups because they acquired more Western education, which resulted in their greater success in the military and civil service. Also, they had the twin talents of business acumen and frontier spirit, which earned them the envy of the other two dominant ethnic nationalities. So when the Igbo led the Easterners in waging the Nigeria-Biafra War, which they lost, the Hausa and the Yoruba took over leadership positions in all areas of Nigerian national life.

The Yoruba have had an enviable position in Nigeria since the end of the war. This is so because from the first time the Igbo were forced out of all other parts of Nigeria and blockaded in Igbo country, the Yoruba took over the high military and civil service positions hitherto occupied by the Igbo. This is in addition to the many positions they had already occupied before the war, for they are also highly educated. Furthermore, they continue to have what none of the other dominant groups have: geographical advantage. Lagos, the political and economic capital of Nigeria, is a Yorubaland. It is the largest seaport in the country and, as it were, the landlord of all foreign countries that have embassies and diplomatic missions in Nigeria. In fact, Lagos enjoys the combined commercial advantage of New York and political advantage of Washington, D.C., in the United States. And when Nigeria engaged in what it called "indiginization" of foreign companies and firms in the country, the Yoruba were its major beneficiaries. The change of Nigerian capital from Lagos to Abuja in the north by Hausa/Fulani military rulers has not changed the situation in any realistic way. In essence, the Yoruba are the most powerful people in contemporary Nigeria.

The Hausa/Fulani people came into the political limelight as the group that led others to defeat the Igbo people in the Nigeria-Biafra War. All the heads of the military juntas that ruled Nigeria from 1967 through 1999 are

Hausa and Fulani except for the two and a half years (1976–79) when General Olusegun Obansanjo held the fort for them as a result of the assassination of General Murtala Mohammed by another Hausa military officer. The war gave the Hausa the opportunity to maintain power undemocratically. They looted the national treasury and entrenched a culture of political corruption and suppression of group and individual liberties in Nigeria. Even when the country came under a civilian regime, the Obasanjo administration was always in constant fear of military coups, which could take place any time the Northerners choose to strike.

The ethnic minority groups from the South South zone of the country, from where Nigeria gets most of its oil wealth, have so mastered the sociopolitical games of the dominant ethnic groups that they constantly play what other Nigerians call the "oil politics" to get whatever they want from the federal government of Nigeria. They were neglected for so long that the violence and disruption of the oil-mining business committed in those areas by their angry youths are crimes that could not be overlooked by any responsible government, as the Obasanjo administration has done. Nevertheless, many people from all ethnic nationalities consider such crimes to be a righteous reaction to decades of deprivations and neglect. But concerned citizens fear that if Nigeria will fight another civil war, it will probably emanate from the South South region.

CULTURE

Language

English is the official language of Nigeria as a result of Britain creating and colonizing the country at the turn of the twentieth century. Since then, the English language has made it possible for the more than four hundred ethnic groups to communicate with one another for purposes of education, administration, commerce, and trade within and outside the country. In addition to English, however, each ethnic group speaks its indigenous Nigerian language, which has many dialects. But a few of the indigenous languages are also widely spoken by nonmembers of their corresponding ethnic groups.

Since the 1960s, Nigeria has been grappling with the multifarious nature of the languages its citizens use functionally. For that reason, the government came up with a language policy that created what is known as "network languages," which are languages recognized according to their indigenous speakers' population figures: Hausa, 23,233,000; Yoruba, 22,571,000; Igbo, 18,434,000; Fulfulde, 9,530,000; Kanuri, 4,498,000; Ibibio, 3,999,000; Tiv,

2,779,000; Ijaw (Izon), 2,171,000; Edo, 1,904,000; Nupe, 1,314,000; Urhobo, 1,274,000; and Igala, 1,160,000. These figures come from Nigeria's 1986 census figures (Table 1.1).

At any rate, the policy did not satisfy all the ethnic minorities. So government went to work again and came up with another policy, which was tagged "Political Distribution of Languages in Nigeria" and which promotes a three-level function in Nigeria: English, the official language; Hausa-Igbo-Yoruba, the national languages; and other local languages. Both language policies were influenced by the stages of political development in the country: English when the country was a colony of Britain; the Hausa, Igbo, and Yoruba languages when the country was divided into Northern Nigeria, Eastern Nigeria, and Western Nigeria; and other local languages following the division of the country into states. Furthermore, the network languages were adopted by the media to serve the information needs of multi-ethnic states, such as Delta, where the citizens of the state could listen to programs in Igbo from Abia, Anambra, Ebonyi, Enugu, or Imo if they are Delta Igbo, or Ijaw if they are Delta Ijaw. What the networks did was to expand the national languages into a few select local languages so as to reach as many audiences as they could, knowing that they could not broadcast in more than four hundred developed and undeveloped languages (Fig. 1.1).

Right from the beginning of the country, every educated Nigerian has been bilingual. Students use English in school and their indigenous languages after

Table 1.1
Nigeria: Population by Language (in descending order)

Nigeria (1986)			
Language	#of Speakers	%	Sub-%
Hausa	23,233,000	22.04	
Yoruba	22,571,000	21.41	60.94
Igbo	18,434,000	17.49	
Fulfulde	9,538,000	9.05	
Kanuri	4,498,000	4.27	
Ibibio	3,999,000	3.79	
Tiv	2,779,000	2.64	
Ijaw (Izon)	2,171,000	2.06	27.18
Edo	1,904,000	1.81	
Nupe	1,314,000	1.25	
Urhobo	1,274,000	1.21	
Igala	1,160,000	1.10	
ts	92,875,000	88.12	
Total 5 tp	105,400,000	100.00	*
df	12,525,000	11.88	

Source: *Journal of the Third World Spectrum* (Spring 1997): 52.

Figure 1.1 Political Distribution of Languages in Nigeria

Three-level Language Function in Nigeria

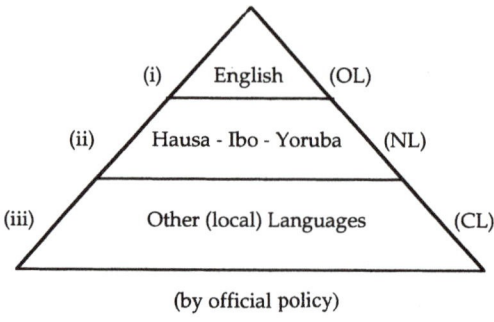

(by official policy)

Source: *Journal of the Third World Spectrum* (Spring 1997): 53.

school hours. Even functional illiterates, such as many subsistence farmers and market women, are bilingual in the sense that they can use either their indigenous languages or pidgin English for communication with nonindigenous traders and businesspeople.

While Hausa is a Chadic language with historical ties to Arabic, Igbo and Yoruba are members of the Kwa language subfamily of West Africa, which was developed as separate languages about 4,500 years ago. However, the languages remained unwritten until the mid-nineteenth century, when the British colonists established mission schools in which missionaries developed Igbo and Yoruba orthographies that enabled them to translate the Bible into those languages. Earlier on, during the northern contact period, Arab Muslim teachers had similarly taught Northerners how to read the Qu'ran, the holy book of Islam, in the Hausa language.

Despite its shortcomings, British colonialism left Nigeria an everlasting legacy: English, an international language of education, commerce, administration, and culture, which not only liberated Nigeria from international isolation but also has managed to unite the multi-ethnic, multicultural peoples of Nigeria.

Religion

Nigerians are deeply religious people who practice their faiths in Christianity, Islam, or one of the many traditional ethnic religions. Also, religion so pervades all aspects of their national life that one wonders from time to time whether Nigeria is indeed a secular state, as the government claims. Besides, there is no separation between church and state.

Christianity is the last of the three organized religions to be introduced and practiced in the country. It was introduced by European missionaries during the southern contact period. Its great influence on the people as well as on government comes from what the church, the school, and the British government did to change the religious beliefs and worldviews of Nigerians, their traditional education, and culture. European Christians used to fight what they saw as ostensible weaknesses in Nigerian ethnic religious practices, including what they characterized as idol worship, sacrifice of twins and ostracization of their mothers, the casting away of patients of deadly diseases like chicken pox to the "evil forest," and branding and discriminating against some people as *untouchables*. The Europeans saw such acts as ungodly and so condemned them. Furthermore, the church welcomed and converted such dregs of society into Christians. That is why such Christians would argue that because of Christianity, the moral compass and worldviews of Nigerians have radically changed for good. Of course, the traditional Nigerians would disagree with such an assertion and would point to the moral decadence, debauchery, and materialistic tendencies of the Nigerian society since the coming of whites to their territories.

In addition, the church and missionary teachers built schools and hospitals to take care of the mind, body, and soul of the Nigerian Christian converts. In the end, many of the converts received training as catechists, interpreters, court clerks, teachers, civil servants, doctors, architects, professors, and politicians. And when the British left the country following Nigeria's attainment of independence, the majority of such mission-trained personnel became the new ruling elite. Also, as a result of the Western education they acquired, the people transformed Nigeria, the erstwhile oral, vernacular society, into a literate and highly educated nation. In addition, through their writings (especially literature and history), the outside world has come to know about Nigerian culture, people, and traditions.

Islam was introduced into Nigeria by Arab Muslims during the northern contact period. The religion was already deeply entrenched for many years in northern parts of the country before the creation of the country. The classic holy wars (Crusades and Jihad), which Christians and Muslims had fought in southern Europe were later fought by British agents (Christians), who advanced from the coastal territories toward the north, and Caliphate Muslims (Arabs), who controlled the northern territories, during the inland contact period. Although the British won those wars, they introduced a system of government they called Indirect Rule (ruling the people through their Muslim chiefs) and allowed them to manage their culture, including their religion, Islam, as long as they accepted the colonial authority of the British. Thus, the country was ruled as if it were two separate countries—Northern Nigeria and Southern Nigeria—until it became Nigeria in 1914.

Because Northern Nigeria, unlike other regions of the country, did not embrace Western education or culture initially, it lagged behind Southern Nigeria, and later in history, behind the Western Region and Eastern Region. The consequence of all that is that the Muslim North does not have the same religious beliefs or worldviews as the Christian South. That is also how the pro-West Southerners came to dominate the pro-Saudi Arabia Northerners academically and educationally. To fight Southern domination in those areas, Northern military officers, who maintained sociopolitical powers for decades in postbellum Nigeria, secretly registered Nigeria as a member of Organization for Islamic Conference (OIC) and received money from Libya and Saudi Arabia to build an Islamic university in Northern Nigeria for the sole purpose of spreading Islamic religion, culture, and civilization in the nation. Today, Muslims have established the Supreme Council for Islamic Affairs as a major government-approved institution.

Each of the ethnic groups in Nigeria had a traditional religion before the coming of Europeans and Arabs. However, the traditional religions became less visible because they did not offer their members the educational and job opportunities that the foreign religions gave to their adherents. Besides, Christianity and foreign education, as well as Western civilization, taught Nigerians to look down upon, even to condemn and abandon, the traditional ethnic religious practices, which are often branded pagan, heathenish, or demonic by those who do not understand them. Yet, in spite of the dominance of the foreign religions, the ethnic religions still have a lot of influence on the belief systems of Nigerians because of their daily encounter with traditional religious practices.

The traditional ethnic religions of Nigeria have various names (e.g., *Esin Ibile* in Yoruba, *Igo Mmuo* in Igbo, and *Bori* in Hausa), but they all are organized around three theological concepts: the greater God (*Olodumare* in Yoruba, *Chukwu* in Igbo, and *Ubangiji* in Hausa); man at three levels of existence (human beings on earth, dead-living ancestors in the spirit world, and unborn children in the womb); and visible and invisible forces. It is a world in which the forces interact, affecting and modifying behavior, including the behavior of human beings and divinities. Such cosmological beliefs make traditional Nigerians respect their fellow human beings, honor their dead-living ancestors (sometimes with sacrifices), treat women with respect (especially pregnant women), and honor the earth (Mother Earth, who protects the ancestors in her womb, which is called "tomb" or "grave") so as to maintain balance and order in the ontological universe. They also treat the environment and all God's creations with reverence and wonderment.

Other Nigerian Cultural Features

In addition to language and religion, there are some other cultural features that characterize Nigerians as a people, as well as demonstrate their affinity with other West African peoples:

- The extended family system, which expresses the notion that a person can be taken care of by relations who act like one's nuclear family. Members of one's extended family may not be related by blood to the one being taken care of. They could be the friends, associates, and fellow villagers of one's parents. Or, they could be distant relatives and grandparents who take over the care of a person if his or her biological parents are poor, dead, or not in a position to help. This ensures that Nigerians do not have to deal with the problem of homelessness. As the Igbo would put it proverbially, "It takes a village to raise a child," and "Helping a *brother* or *sister* to get up."

- Rituals and ceremonies, which emanate from traditional religious observances and worldviews that have been secularized. The ritual of "breaking of kola nut," for instance, was originally a way of honoring the dead-living ancestors, which involves invoking their presence with palm wine, kola nut, and white clay before meals, during family and village meetings, and when one has visitors. In its secular form, the ritual has become an item in the agenda of public ceremonies, such as weddings, naming of children and age-grades (to be discussed in Chapter 3), political rallies, conferences, and taking of titles. The idea is that the ancestors and the unborn children in the womb are part and parcel of the ethnic community; therefore, the secularized rituals have continued to retain a religious streak and ambiance.

- Folk dances, which are one of the ethnic rituals that have now become secular celebrations. For example, Dance of the Maidens, once preformed during sessions of sacrifice and blessing of a newly married couple, has become one of the regularly staged dances during political and other social events. All ethnic groups have their chosen dances during village, clan, or state events, such as political rallies and art festivals. During such occasions, masquerade dancers, who represent spirit beings, cultic and titular orders, and other esoteric organizations, usually mix freely with ordinary citizens in festive celebrations.

- Festivals, which Nigerians celebrate yearly, quarterly, and biannually. They include the New Yam Festival, originally staged to honor ritualistically the Earth-goddess in charge of human, animal, and plant fertility. However, the New Yam Festival has since become a secular event celebrated with a lot of folk dances. Also, there are some annual traditional Nigerian festivals that coincide with the celebrations of Christian and Islamic religious observances. For instance, the second Yam Harvest Festival coincides with Christmas celebration in Igboland. That means that both events create a festive atmosphere in which Christians and non-Christians express gratitude to their God or gods and goddesses in songs and dances. Often, their religious significance is forgotten as their celebrative and entertainment values become the focus.

- Food, including pounded yam *foofoo* (doughballs) dipped in *egusi* (melon), okra, or *ogbono* soup (cooked with smoked fish, stockfish, and a variety of meat, and often spiced with hot red pepper, onions, and other ingredients). Rice, beans, plantain, bananas, yam, cocoyam, *garri,* and carrots form the menu of regular meals. *Akamu* or *ogi, akara,* corn, and fried plantain are regularly served as breakfast. And since the building of the Kainji Dam in the north, Nigerians have had a regular supply of seafood that complements their standard recipes.

- Art, fashion, music, and body makeup, which are the means through which Nigerians of all ethnic extractions express their group identity. The individual groups are easily identified by the facial marks and scarifications they bear and by the body decorations and the traditional clothes they wear. Hats, anklets, ox tail, and hand fans they carry also indicate the chieftaincy titles they have earned, especially in the southern states. Carved doors, images of spirit beings, masks, raffia garb, and iron and earthen wares, which are made for decorative and ornamentation purposes go a long way to characterize Nigerians as creative and artistic people. Their songs and music, both those played for celebrations and worship as well as those produced for trade, are an aspect of the popular West African Juju music, High life, and reggae rhythms.

To sum up, the various elements of culture that have been presented constitute a springboard from which each generation of Nigerian immigrants begins its adaptation and adjustment processes in a new land; it is a wellspring from whence they draw the strength they need in order to survive and to make their peculiar contributions to the American national life. Why and how this new group of immigrants came to the United States are discussed in the next chapter.

PART II

COMING TO THE UNITED STATES

2

Nigerian Immigration to the United States: An Overview

According to U.S. Census Bureau reports, 25,528 Nigerians lived in the United States in 1980, and by 1990, that figure had increased to 91,688 (of which 55,350 are immigrants). Judging from the steady rise in the number of Nigerian immigrants admitted annually into this country since then, it is estimated that the 2000 census figures currently under review by the bureau could put the population of Nigerian Americans above 100,000. Before 1980, however, neither the Census Bureau nor the Immigration and Naturalization Service (INS) had any records of the Nigerians as a separate group of immigrants from Africa. Instead, what they both have is a record of a combined figure of immigrants from all African countries, which begins with only one immigrant in 1820 and ends with 28,954 in 1970—a figure that is less than that of one Asian country, the Philippines, whose immigrant population figure was 98,376 in 1970.

This chapter gives an overview of Nigerian immigration to the United States, discussing such factors as when Nigerians began to immigrate, why they came, what their circumstances and general background were in their native land, and reasons for their return migration.

GENERAL BACKGROUND OF NIGERIAN IMMIGRATION

Essentially, the history of Nigerian immigration to the United States is about Nigerian students' quests for Western education, which occurred in the first three of the following four periods: the early colonial period (1925–52);

the late colonial period (1952–60); the postcolonial period (1961–70); and the postbellum period (1970 and after), which refers to the aftermath of the Nigeria-Biafra War.

As noted in Chapter 1, Nigeria was not formally a country until 1914, and the only contacts its citizens made with the outside world happened along the southern coastal lines and within the northern borders of the country, between the fifteenth and nineteenth centuries. That means that until those dates, the country was very much a closed society. In addition, the Nigerian territories were very rich in human and natural resources. For that reason, its citizens did not need to go outside of its borders to look for jobs. Also, they did not engage in internal and international wars when the British were still in charge of their national affairs. Hence there was no need for them to flee the country in search of freedom, employment opportunities, or asylum like their Asian counterparts.

Furthermore, because such surface and general causes of immigration did not apply to them initially, Nigerians were neither much affected by, nor aware of, the various U.S. immigration laws that affected other new immigrants, including the passage of the Immigration Act of 1965, which liberalized immigration conditions for any groups of immigrants wanting to come to the United States, until the outbreak of their civil war, which forced some people to flee the country after 1970. At any rate, the majority of them were college students. That explains in part why the U.S. Census Bureau and the Immigration and Naturalization Service did not have a significant enough number of Nigerian immigrants to necessitate the creation of separate census and immigration figures for them (and other individual sub-Saharan African countries) until 1980 (Table 2.1).

Table 2.1
Selected Foreign-Born Population from West Africa, 1980 and 1990

Country	1990	1980
Ghana	20,889	7,564
Liberia	11,455	3,728
Nigeria	55,350	25,528
Senegal	2,287	762
Sierra Leone	7,217	1,963
Total	97,198	39,545

Source: U.S. Bureau of the Census, Technical Paper 29–Table 3: Region and Country or Area of Birth of the Foreign Born, 1960 to 1990.

CAUSES AND CHARACTERISTICS
OF NIGERIAN IMMIGRATION

The overall Nigerian immigration to the United States, which occurred in four periods, was occasioned by such issues as the need for American education, the horrible sociopolitical situation in Nigeria, and the aftermath of the Nigerian civil war, as well as military dictatorships of the 1980s and 1990s. Each of these issues had their peculiar influences on the decisions of those who came to the United States in all four periods, which are discussed here.

The First Period of Immigration (1925–52)

During the first period of immigration, Nigeria was under British colonial rule. For that reason, its citizens were British subjects, and anyone who wanted to travel overseas needed to have a British passport or visa. Students who needed higher education were encouraged to go to British institutions foremost or to any other institutions of higher learning within the British Commonwealth. However, in spite of all the restrictions placed on Nigerians who wanted to go elsewhere, a small group of students, including Nnamdi Azikiwe, Mazi Mbonu Ojike, and Hogan Edem Ani-Okokon, managed to come to the United States for their higher education. In the process, they became the first group of Nigerian immigrants to the United States. But they did not come to settle. In fact, the story of Azikiwe serves as a paradigm of all waves of Nigerian immigration in the United States up to the third period.

Born in Zungeru in Northern Nigeria to Igbo parents in 1904, Azikiwe attended mission schools in Onitsha, Lagos, and Calabar before traveling to Lagos for further education in 1921. After serving for a while as a government clerk in the Treasury Office in Lagos, he came to the United States in 1925. He enrolled in Storer College, but soon transferred to Howard University in Washington, D.C., and subsequently to Lincoln University in Pennsylvania, from where he graduated. After graduation, he lectured in political science at Lincoln University and obtained his postgraduate degrees from Columbia University and the University of Pennsylvania. His return to Nigeria at the end of 1934 marks the first reported case of Nigerian return migration.

What Azikiwe did with his American experience greatly influenced other Nigerians in deciding to come to the United States. After one year of his return to Nigeria, Azikiwe moved to Accra in Ghana, West Africa, where in 1935 he became editor of the Accra *African Morning Post*. In 1938 he returned to Nigeria, where he established the newspaper *West African Pilot*, whose motto was, "Show the light and the people will find their way." After a period of political activity in the Nigerian Youth Movement, he joined with Herbert Macaulay to found a political party, the National Council of Nigeria and the Cameroons (NCNC). From that time on, through journalism and political leadership, he fought consistently for the greatness of Africa and for her citizens everywhere (Azikiwe 1970, vi–vii). In fact, his roles in the formation of the Pan-African Movement as well as his collaborative work with other great African political leaders and heads of state like Kwame Nkrumah of Ghana, Julius Nyerere of Tanzania, and David Arop Moi of Kenya in fighting and winning political independence for African nations earned Azikiwe the praise name "Zik of Africa."

From 1954 to 1959, Azikiwe was Premier of Eastern Region of Nigeria. In December 1959, he resigned from that office and was in January 1960 elected President of the Senate. On November 16, 1960, he served as the first indigenous governor-general of the Federation of Nigeria, and was thereafter elected the first President of the Federal Republic of Nigeria on October 1, 1963.

Empowered by the American education he received, by American notion of liberty in all aspects of people's individual and group life that he admired, and by his personal courage, charisma, and nationalistic feelings, Azikiwe led other Nigerian patriots to challenge the British colonial authorities in London, which effort eventually led to Nigeria's attainment of political independence.

Nnamdi Azikiwe and his wife.

His influence caused other Nigerian students to come to the United States and become empowered just like Zik of Africa. In the end, more students decided to come to the United States for their higher education than those who went to Europe for what was then popularly called the "Golden Fleece."

In the meantime, Great Britain had established in 1948 the University College, Ibadan, in Nigeria as a campus of London University. The Nigerian students enrolled in it were trained solely to become teachers, administrators, and civil servants after graduation so as to perpetuate British educational and civil service systems, and to inculcate its culture and civilization in Nigerians, without much regard for their indigenous sociocultural and religious institutions.

The Second Period of Immigration (1952–60)

The group of students immigrating to the United States during the second period of immigration was more diverse than the first group. It included some graduates of Ibadan who were coming for graduate studies. That meant that they were more mature, knew what university life involved, and were academically ready to face and appreciate various aspects of American education and life in general. Also, because of the college degrees they acquired before coming, it was easy for them to find jobs on university campuses or outside of them with special permission from the INS through the offices of their foreign students directors. The result was that some of them chose to stay behind and settle in the United States, while others returned to Nigeria to occupy elevated positions in high schools, colleges, and the civil service.

Other student immigrants came from high schools and teacher training colleges with the sponsorships of mission school authorities and churches. While many of them returned to Nigeria after graduation to help build and expand the mission schools and churches that sponsored them, a few of them managed to stay back in the United States, thereby swelling the number of Nigerians there.

During this time, Nigerians had begun to see the benefits of Western education in their country. For that reason, more and more parents were encouraged to send their children to high schools and teacher training colleges. More schools and colleges were built to accommodate them, and that in itself created more job openings for college graduates. Also, because the country, whose population was about 55,000,000 in 1958, had only one university college, it was impossible to absorb all the qualified Nigerian university candidates in one institution. To the more enthusiastic ones, however, American institutions became readily available alternatives to the British and other Commonwealth institutions that could not, and would not, admit Nigerians who had applied to them for college education.

This third group of student immigrants in the United States constituted a larger portion of those who decided to settle in the United States after their schooling, for they were not forced by either the government or the church to return to Nigeria to serve those who sponsored them. Instead, they stayed in the United States to work and to send some of the money they made to their parents and private sponsors, whom they visited occasionally in Nigeria. Many of them quickly adapted to the American way of life. In fact, some of them got married to Americans, who facilitated their applications for U.S. citizenship.

Even though many Nigerians came to the United States for higher education, two factors prevented more of them from coming: The first is that the British were in control of higher education and immigration matters in Nigeria. For that reason, they restricted the number of passports issued to Nigerians traveling outside of the country for whatever purpose, because they regarded such persons as their subjects. Besides, the British did not like the messages that Azikiwe and his fellow graduates of American universities were sending to their countrymen and -women, which urged them to fight for their political freedom from their colonial master, Great Britain. In fact, to the British, allowing more Nigerians to receive American education was tantamount to tacit encouragement of Nigerian students' postgraduation opposition of British rule and empire.

The second factor was the war of propaganda that the British waged against American life and education. Some of the British agents would tell Nigerian high school students that Americans were malcontents (a covert reference to the American War of Independence they fought to free themselves against British colonial rule) and that their life was generally crude and uncouth. Resultantly, some of the Nigerian graduates of American universities were discriminated against by British agents when they applied for work in the Nigerian civil service system, because such agents preferred diplomas obtained from either British or Commonwealth universities to those obtained from American institutions. Additionally, the British offered Commonwealth scholarships to Nigerians to study abroad. But all those measures the British took to discourage Nigerians from coming to receive American higher education were soon ended by two historic events that took place in 1960: Nigeria's attainment of independence and the establishment of its first indigenous university.

The Third Period of Immigration (1960–70)

This third period of Nigerian immigration in the United States was marked by momentous events that took place both in Nigeria and the

United States. The first of them is Nigeria's attainment of political independence in 1960, which radically changed the status of its people from being British subjects to free citizens of Nigeria. From that historic date, the destiny of Nigeria lay in the hands of Nigerians. They had their own passport offices that issued them passports to travel wherever they pleased in the world. Also, qualified Nigerians could apply to the American Embassy in Lagos for a visa to travel to any American universities and colleges that offered them admissions. The more such students were granted visas to come to the United States, the more inspiration they gave others to join them. Within a few years, the number of Nigerian students in the United States increased significantly.

Also the attainment of independence caused British administrators and agents to leave Nigeria for their home country, thus creating more job opportunities for qualified Nigerians. Simultaneously, as more Nigerians left for the United States for further studies, others who had graduated from American universities returned to Nigeria and took over some of the jobs hitherto held by the British. Their performance on the job gave the lie to the British propaganda leveled against American education and civilization.

The second historic event that had a very positive effect on Nigerian immigration to the United States took place in November 1960, when the first indigenous Nigerian university, the University of Nigeria, Nsukka, in Eastern Nigeria, opened its doors to Nigerian students. The founder was Nnamdi Azikiwe, who collaborated with Michigan State University administrators to build the young institution. Both the curricular offerings and the professors and administrators were mainly American. At first, the British-educated Nigerian civil servants and educators then in charge of higher education in Nigeria were very skeptical of the type and quality of education being offered to the students at Nsukka. To the amazement of such skeptics, however, the first group of Nsukka graduates beat the Ibadan "boys" in national civil service exams. Their strength was due in part to the general studies program that the university offered to them: a program that broadened their education and went beyond their individual majors. Indeed the American system was at variance with the British system, which produced majors of given disciplines who could not deal very intellectually with issues outside their areas of specialization. And yet, as a young country, Nigeria needed all-round officers who could deal with myriads of national problems that the citizens faced on attainment of independence. So for the first time ever, more and more people began ranking American education a little higher than that of the British. And such a positive appraisal further encouraged more Nigerians to come to the United States for higher education.

But the momentous external event that made the largest and most lasting impact on the general life of educated Nigerians as well as indirectly causing more Nigerian immigration to the United States was the launching of the Peace Corps program by President John F. Kennedy in 1961. That program, which was dubbed "the bold experiment" (Rice 1965), was intended to achieve three goals: to provide the developing countries with trained manpower, to help promote a better understanding of Americans on the part of the peoples served, and to help increase American knowledge of other peoples and cultures. Nigeria, Tanzania, and Ghana were the first three sub-Saharan African countries that the Peace Corps men and women served. In 1962, 100 of them began their service in Nigeria. This service could not have come at a better time for Nigerian social and economic development.

First, on attainment of independence, the new Nigerian Ministry of Education had incorporated the many colonial mission schools and colleges without the necessary complementary indigenous faculty to teach those courses that the foreign personnel had taught during the colonial days. Some of the Peace Corps volunteers worked in some of the understaffed schools, collaborating on a practical basis with experienced church professionals without what Rice (1965) refers to as "religious proselytizing or propagandizing," so as to maintain the spirit of separation of church and state. Furthermore, the volunteers offered technical, managerial, and other skilled labor, such as doctors, nurses, road overseers, and bankers, that Nigeria was in dire need of. To Nigerians, the Peace Corps volunteers' services achieved the first two goals of the program in the sense that, while providing the people with the much-needed manpower, the volunteers in a practical manner gave Nigerians a better view of American national and individual life, which the British had attempted seriously to obscure through their propaganda machinery during the colonial days. The volunteers were prepared to endure the following:

> You will live in a small wooden house, sleep on the floor on a bamboo mat, with a pillow stuffed with rice grain and a mosquito net to protect you from the swarms of bloodthirsty mosquitoes. The heavy, humid heat and the hard bed will not be comfortable...you will suffer from the damp weather...leeches will cling to you; worms, frogs and snakes will be numerous. (Rice 1965, 70)

They did so in order to know the people well, and in turn, the Nigerians would have the opportunity to see them at work at very close range. Hence the third goal of the program was accomplished.

Second, the Peace Corps volunteers endured all that through sheer toughness of spirit, which emanates from what is often called the American "frontier spirit," and their altruistic sacrifice to help those who were less fortunate than they; above all, they were taking up President Kennedy's challenge, "Ask not what the country can do for you—ask what you can do for the country." From seeing all that, educated Nigerians, who had been socially stratified and set aside from other Nigerians by British education, were somehow humbled by the American sense of patriotism and altruism and dignity of labor, as well as by the idea of the American dream. So some of them decided to come to the United States not only to receive American higher education but also to learn more about other American sociopolitical, educational, economic, and banking systems. Besides, the Peace Corps volunteers explained to the Nigerian youths about various educational and economic opportunities that existed in the United States and helped them with visa applications. That way, the floodgates of immigration were opened to those who were qualified and could afford to come to the United States from 1961 until 1967, when the Nigerian civil war began.

The war severely affected the immigration ambitions of Nigerians from Eastern Nigeria, which was then called Biafra, but other Nigerians in the Midwest, Western Nigeria, and Northern Nigeria were free to travel if they satisfied American immigration requirements, which the American Embassy in Lagos verified. Nevertheless, Peace Corps volunteers who served in Eastern Nigeria before the war and knew how obsessed Easterners were with attainment of higher education often maintained links with Easterners all through the war. They did so by sending the Biafrans letters and educational materials through Caritas International and World Council of Churches, which rendered humanitarian services to Biafra. At the end of the war, the "pen pal" link that the Peace Corps volunteers maintained enabled them to trace some of the surviving Biafrans in order to sponsor their higher education in the United States.

The Fourth Period of Immigration (1970 and After)

As soon as the war ended, religious organizations, such as Catholic Relief Services, Caritas International, the World Council of Churches, Seventh Day Adventist Church, and the Presbyterian Church, as well as other humanitarian organizations, brought food, medicine, and clothing to the sick and starved ex-Biafran children and the aged. They saw horrors of war first hand; they heard stories of inhumanity directly; and they left with heavy hearts, thinking of what further help they could give to the victims of the war. In the end, those religious organizations that had affiliations with Nigerian institutions sponsored the immigration of their members to the United States. Also, Nigerians living in the United States while the Nigeria-Biafra War raged visited home, appraised the situation on the ground, and brought back with them to the United States as many relatives as the American Embassy would allow. So for the first time in Nigeria history, war became the cause of immigration, and more students from the war-ravaged Eastern Nigeria easily made good cases for their immigration to the United States, as long as they had good academic qualifications and credible sponsors or verifiable means of financial support.

The gloomy sociopolitical and economic conditions in Nigeria resulting from their civil war were so unbearable for Easterners that everybody wanted to flee the country, if they had the opportunity and means of doing so. More and more Nigerian single men and women living in the United States briefly came to their native Igboland to marry, with a view to producing children who could help replace the more than one million Igbo people massacred before, during, and after the war in Northern and South South Nigeria. It was during this period that the new Immigration Act, enacted in 1965, was used to advantage by some Nigerian Americans applying for the travel visas of their spouses, children, parents, and siblings they left behind in Nigeria. By the year 1980, the hitherto negligible number of Nigerian immigrants in the United States rose to 25,528.

The military dictatorships that emerged during and after the war caused the sociopolitical and economic conditions of Nigerians from every region, state, and ethnic or gender group (with the exception of the military and their families) to worsen. There was abuse of power and denial of fundamental human rights, including freedom of speech. In fact, a few courageous Nigerians, like the media practitioners and college professors, who spoke against the various military juntas' abuse of power and despotism, were reportedly assassinated or imprisoned, and the general public was cowed to a point where they merely existed instead of living as fulfilled human beings. The rule of law was replaced with military decrees, and university administrators and professors were told by the military how they should govern and teach students on their campuses. Above all, college professors and students could no longer order the academic books and equipment they needed for their academic and professional growth. In the end, many of them made the decision to leave the country, if they could. Before the government and parents could realize what had happened to Nigerian education, there was a dearth of trained personnel in the educational institutions, which government authorities dubbed "brain drain." There was a mass exodus of professors leaving for foreign countries, and those who had received higher degrees from American universities came back to teach in the United States. Their numbers swelled the population of Nigerians already here in the United States from 25,528 in 1980 to 55,350 in 1990.

The sordid sociopolitical and economic conditions in Nigeria degenerated even further in the last decade of the twentieth century, as the various military juntas continued to oust and replace one another. In the process, they killed and imprisoned civilians who ran for elective political offices, until the United States helped Nigerian authorities to conduct elections that ushered in a democratically elected government on May 29, 1999, headed by Olusegun Obasanjo. Ostensibly, Nigerians started from then to exercise freedom of speech and to take part in electing those who governed them at the federal, state, and local levels. However, it should be noted that there were more cases of armed robbery, civil unrest, and killing of people within the first two years of the Obasanjo regime than there were during the first ten years of military rules after the war. The rate of inflation was 300 percent, and the Nigerian currency, the naira (₦), whose value was ₦1 (one naira) to $2 (two U.S. dollars) in 1982, became so worthless that $1 (one U.S. dollar) exchanged for ₦136.80 in April of 2001. As a result, only the ex-military officers, ruling government officials, some corrupt business men and women, and drug traffickers were able to absorb the effects of inflation and abject poverty in 2001 Nigerian society.

Many blamed Obasanjo personally for their sorry situations in contemporary Nigerian society. They argued that, although he was elected as a civilian president, he ruled as the retired military general he was before contesting election as a civilian; that Obasanjo had not totally gotten rid of the military culture he acquired over the years in terms of style of governance, nor had he been able to deal with the corruption and debauchery that characterized the various military regimes before his civilian administration. That criticism is exemplified in a June 6, 2001, Nigerian *Vanguard Online Edition,* where a founding father of the Peoples Democratic Party (PDP)—Obasanjo's ruling political party—Suleiman Kumo, was reported to have lamented that his "party which was formed to fight dictatorship of any kind and promote democracy" had failed because both the party and the president had not upheld the characteristics of true democracy:

Democracy necessitates two things—number one is a credible electoral system: democracy is founded upon free and fair and honest elections through the party and the three levels of government, but these have been denied in the PDP. Number two: democracy is founded upon the pillar of freedom of speech, defense, and association even in the party.

But in the case of Nigeria, democracy can only survive and thrive if political parties take their responsibilities seriously and see themselves as the vehicles of promoting democracy; but the PDP is not above the executive or the legislature because *Obasanjo has been accustomed to the military style of government which is the only thing he knows* [emphasis added]. From the moment he became president, he [Obasanjo] started taking steps to bring under his control and domination both the party and the legislature. He ensured the emergence of those he could manipulate as leaders of the national assembly. (http://www.vanguardngr.com/04062001/R3060601.htm)

These social, political, economic, and security problems, as well as poor governance eventuated in the general denial of group and individual liberties to the citizens, which in turn created a new wave of Nigerian immigrants in the United States. That is, they were seeking political asylum, economic freedom, and civil liberties, unlike the first group, whose primary ambition was to acquire American higher education. Their presence increased the Nigerian American population significantly (Table 2.2).

Characteristics of Nigerian Immigration

Now that we have examined the major surface causes of Nigerian immigration to the United States, we need to know also the composition, characteristics, and settlement patterns of those who made the decision to come to our country.

First of all, it should be noted that all Nigerian immigrants in the United States should be regarded as the new immigrants, because they did not come until 1925.

Table 2.2
Nigerian Immigrants Admitted in the United States, Fiscal Years 1988–98

Year	Population
1988	3,343
1989	5,213
1990	8,843
1991	7,912
1992	4,551
1993	4,448
1994	3,950
1995	6,818
1996	10,221
1997	7,038
1998	7,746

Source: *1998 Statistical Yearbook of the INS*, Table 3.

The implication of this fact is that the characteristics of the immigrants in any of the four immigration periods described previously are virtually similar, just as the causes of their immigration to the United States are virtually the same.

Admission by Age. The INS records show that nonimmigrant Nigerians admitted by age range from children under fifteen years old through adults who are sixty-five years and older. However, the thirty-five to forty-four age bracket is the largest, and those who fall in it number 10,306. They are followed by the forty-five to sixty-four age group, which numbers 9,033. And the third largest group falls within the twenty-five to thirty-four age bracket, numbering 8,619 (Table 2.3).

Admission by Sponsorship. The INS uses certain preferential sponsorships as a factor in admitting the immigrants. They include family sponsorship, employment-based preference, immediate relationships to U.S. citizens, and refugee and asylum adjustments, as well as a diversity program. For the fiscal year 1998, the preferential sponsorship criteria favored Diversity Program applicants (3,185) and Spouses of Immigrants (1,828) over and above the other factors (Table 2.4).

Admission by Major Occupation. A large number of Nigerians seeking immigration to the United States every year are relatively highly educated. For that reason, many of them come to the United States with job offers already in hand, and they come to serve as professionals and executives in their chosen areas of specialization. That is why they always top the lists of Nigerians admitted into this country every year. For example, in fiscal year 1998, 1,286 persons out of a total of 2,907 admitted under the Major Occupation category came under the Professional Specialty and Technical subcategory.

It should be noted that, of the 4,839 persons classified as having no occupation or their occupation not reported, many were college students who

Table 2.3
Nonimmigrant Nigerians Admitted by Age, Fiscal Year 1998

Ages	Number of Nonimmigrants Admitted
Under 15 years	3,429
15-19	1,412
20-24	1,509
25-34	8,619
35-34	10,306
45-64	9,033
65 years and over	1,609
Unknown	12
All Ages	35,929

Source: *1998 Statistical Yearbook of the INS*, Table 42.

Table 2.4

Admission of Nigerian Immigrants by Sponsorship, Fiscal Year 1998

Family-sponsored Preference		344
Employment-based Preference		631
Immediate Relatives of Citizens:		
Spouses	1,828	
Children	721	
Parents	906	
Total Relatives		3,455
Refugee and Asylum Adjustments		112
Diversity Program		3,185
IRCA Legalization		3
Cancellation of Removal		4
Other		12
Total		7,746

Source: *1998 Statistical Yearbook of the INS*, Table 8.

worked part-time and those who took up jobs after graduation without reporting their occupation to the INS. In other words, the record, such as we have here, reflects Nigerian immigrants' preadmission working status, which changes radically once they come to settle in the United States (Table 2.5).

Settlement Patterns. Before the Nigerian immigrants are granted visas, they already have in mind ideal places they intend to live in the United States. From the statistics shown in Table 2.6, one can tell that they prefer living in the southern states, where the climate is warmer and costs of living and of education are generally lower than they are in the Northeast and

Table 2.5

Nigerian Immigrants Admitted by Major Occupation, Fiscal Year 1998

Occupation	Number
Professional Specialty and Technical	1,286
Executive, Administrative, and Managerial	180
Sales	432
Administrative Support	294
Precision Production, Craft, and Repair	79
Operator, Fabricator, and Laborer	83
Farming, Forestry, and Fishing	66
Services	487
Occupational Total	2907
No Occupation or Not Reported	4,839
Admission Total	7,746

Source: *1998 Statistical Yearbook of the INS*, Table 8.

Table 2.6
Nigerian Immigrants Admitted by States of Intended Residence, Fiscal Year 1998

States in Order of Preference	Population
New York	1,301
Texas	1,008
Maryland	994
California	653
New Jersey	568
Georgia	516
Illinois	418
Florida	248
Massachusetts	202
Michigan	194
Minnesota	172
North Carolina	153
Pennsylvania	148
District of Columbia	125

Source: *1998 Statistical Yearbook of the INS*, Table 17.

Northwest. Besides the weather and cost of living, such immigrants consider cities and states that are liberal in allowing them to work (with or without official permits) to support themselves and their families while attending college. However, when they come in, they adjust their preferences to suit practically their educational needs. After they have received the education and acquired the qualifications necessary for the high-paying jobs they desire, they move to any part of the country where such jobs are and settle down as Americans.

Return Migration. Nigerian return migration from the United States was a frequent trend from 1935 through 1963 because the pioneer Nigerian immigrants came primarily for acquisition of American higher education. So, upon graduation, they quickly returned to occupy lucrative positions in government, churches, and schools in Nigeria. Also, some of them, like Azikiwe, began their own private enterprises. In addition, the establishment of more schools and colleges in postindependence Nigeria created unprecedented job opportunities for the returnee graduates. However, the return migration trend was somehow slowed down by the civil war, although it picked up again as a result of the boom in Nigerian oil industry, from 1975 to 1985.

Neither the Nigerian immigration authority nor the United States Immigration and Naturalization Service has a record of voluntary return migrations, because Nigerians are generally reluctant to respond to interviews and surveys that require them to talk about their immigration status or other personal matters. What the INS has, though, is a record of aliens removed by criminal status of selected countries of nationality, including Nigeria (Table 2.7).

In the end, some of the immigrants who returned voluntarily between 1975 and 1985 include those who later engaged in reverse return migration. In other words, after they returned from the United States to Nigeria, they left Nigeria again and went back to the United States as a result of the Nigerian military juntas' activities, which made life too unbearable for the people, as discussed previously. In fact, the highest number of nonimmigrants (10,306) admitted to the United States came in 1996, a year that marked the height of General Sani Abacha's dictatorial regime. This time, many of the Nigerians finally decided to become U.S. citizens through naturalization.

In sum, although Nigerian immigration to the United States began in 1925 and took place in four periods, its causes in those periods are virtually the same: the people's incessant yearning for American higher education and their ambition to escape the sordid social, economic, and political situations in Nigeria. Such conditions emanated from the civil war and its aftermath, which ushered in the various military dictatorships and misrule by the despotic governments of the 1980s and 1990s. Added to those internal stimuli was the external one, which began in the 1960s: the American Peace Corps program, which taught not only the notions of the American dream and frontier spirit but also what it meant for any Nigerians coming to the United States to live in freedom as individuals or groups. In the end, the Nigerians came, saw, and enjoyed the realities of the general American life, as well as its social, economic, and political institutions. While some of the admitted Nigerians voluntarily returned to their native land after a while, others were deported because of the criminal and noncriminal offenses they committed. However, those who decided and were qualified to remain in the United States had to make some adjustments in order to adapt to the new social order. How they live in their new land is the subject of Part III.

Table 2.7
Nigerians Removed by Criminal/Noncriminal Status, Fiscal Years 1993–98

Year	Criminal	Non-criminal	Total
1993	262	73	335
1994	404	86	490
1995	261	71	332
1996	244	70	314
1997	251	144	395
1998	283	206	489

Source: *1998 Statistical Yearbook of the INS*, Table 66.

PART III

ADJUSTMENT AND ADAPTATION

3

Dropping the Cultural Baggage

The Nigerian immigrants who come to live in the United States bring some cultural baggage that sometimes clashes with the U.S. culture. Quite often, the cultural areas where there might be some friction are family values, ethnic associations, folkways, religion, bilingualism, attitudes toward education, and political culture. Initially, the tension between the old and the new cultures creates some cultural shock in the newcomers, but with proper orientation and a positive attitude, they are able to embrace the emerging culture. All that is a social change process, which involves adjustment to, and adaptation of, the American national culture.

This chapter explores the Nigerian immigrants' cultural baggage and how they attempt to modify their premigration culture so as to adapt to all cultural aspects of their new society.

PREMIGRATION FAMILY STRUCTURE AND TRADITIONAL INSTITUTIONS

A typical traditional Nigerian family is polygamous in structure—meaning that it comprises a man (who is the head of the family), at least two wives, and many children. Reasons for the many wives and children can be found in their social, economic, religious, moral, and security institutions, as well as matters of inheritance, all of which are briefly discussed in the following sections.

Social Structure

The social structure of each of the Nigerian indigenous communities is complicated; however, at the base of that structure is the village, which comprises families and compounds. Usually, a village is founded by one man and his wife or wives who live in a compound, which is comprised of a main building (called *obi* in Igbo) for the man and smaller structures (which the British called "huts" when they colonized Nigeria) for the wives. As the family grows (through the birth of children and the marrying of more wives) the compound is expanded to accommodate adult male children and grandchildren and their wives. In time, the male descendants of the original founder of the compound would, in turn, found their own compounds until an aggregation of the compounds becomes a village. It is in the microcosmic society of the families and the macrocosmic society of the villages that the worldview, customs, mores, and ethos of the people are handed down orally from one generation to another, because all Nigerian societies were oral cultures before the coming of the whites. Also, the village is the platform from which all the social institutions, such as marriage, religion, politics, traditional education, culture, and customs, are orally transmitted to and imbibed by the citizens. To date, the village continues to serve as the conscience of the people, even when Western civilization and forces of urbanization have modified and mediated some of the behaviors of postcolonial Nigerian societies. In essence, if a man did not marry many wives and have many children (especially males), founding the compounds and villages would be a slow, if not an impossible, process.

Economic Structure

The economic system of all primordial Nigerian societies was structured around subsistence farming and petty trading, both of which were, and still are, labor-intensive because of lack of mechanized agricultural and commercial systems. For that reason, men needed to marry many wives and raise many children who constituted the labor force on the farmlands. Also, some of them were employed to convey their farm produce, artwork, and other material wares from one village market to another on foot. The implication of all that is that the more wives and children a man had, the greater the chances he had to becoming rich and wealthy. And, from his wealth and riches, he was able to acquire titles that put him in the higher echelon of their highly stratified societies.

Religious Structure

Each of the indigenous Nigerian ethnic religions is *polytheistic,* meaning having many gods. The practice involves the use of many males as priests and men avoiding sexual intercourse with nursing women, as well as women not cooking for their husbands or visiting their *obi* when they are having their menstrual period, so as to avoid desecrating the family shrines and altars. Because of these factors, men who can afford it are free to marry many wives, who take turns in cooking for them when any of them is "impure," and sleep with those who are not nursing babies. Although this is disadvantageous for women, it was a common practice in all primordial societies of West Africa. Christianity and Western education have since joined forces to modify the religious behavior of the modern Nigerian.

Moral and Ethical Structure

The moral and ethical structure of the traditional Nigerians is informed by their religious beliefs and worldviews. Because every village comprises descendants of one founder, such descendants regard themselves as "brothers" and "sisters" or "cousins." For that reason, they do not marry each other for fear of committing incest. Also, adultery and fornication between citizens of the same village are condemned not just as immoral behavior but also as an incestuous relationship. And citizens are taught to tell the truth always, whether or not they are under oath, for they believe that the watchful eyes of the dead-living ancestors (who are not limited by time and space) are always upon them, and every crime, whether seen or unseen, known or unknown by fellow human beings, is usually punished. So every villager tries his or her best to avoid social offenses or treating fellow villagers unjustly and unkindly. But if they do fall off the mark of acceptable moral behavior, they normally seek the forgiveness of their fellow men and women and their gods and goddesses, as well as their dead-living ancestors through the offer of propitiatory sacrifices.

Security Structure

Every village or clan was responsible for their own security, which was solely the men's job. They raised strong young men as constabulary, militia, and soldiers, to guard the villages, farmlands, and barns, to protect women, children, and old and sick men, and to fight intervillage and intertribal wars. Usually, each family was required to send their male children to serve in those paramilitary forces. If a man could not send any of his children when they were needed because they were all female, he felt inadequate and unfulfilled. He could be prevented from enjoying certain social privileges accorded only to men whose children have served in the armed forces. So, to avoid being deprived in any way, such a man would resort to marrying more women with the hope that any of the wives could bear him male children. Of course, the pressure to marry more women was more on the husbands of barren women. To date, divorcing either barren women or mothers of girls only is culturally out of the question. Instead, such women encourage their husbands to marry other women or, in some cases, rich women find and pay the bride price of other women for their husbands, in hopes of getting male children who are expected to further strengthen, enrich, and expand their family and compound. Children of such a family are expected to treat all the women in the household as their biological mother, regardless of who bore whom. Hence, the spirit of group-caring and group-sharing is instilled in Nigerians (especially Igbo children) at a very young age.

Matters of Inheritance

In traditional Nigerian societies, marriage is both *patrilocal*, meaning that the family is situated in the man's home or compound, and *patrilineal*, meaning that the family inheritance comes through the man's line of the family. This is because Nigeria is a patriarchal society. Furthermore, the headship of the individual families, or the governance of the village or clan is given to the first son of the family, the oldest in the compound, village, or clan, when the ruling elder or patriarch dies.

Changes in Premigration Nigerian Family Structure and Traditional Institutions

As a result of the coming of the colonialist whites into Nigeria, the erstwhile traditional Nigerian family structure (which was, in the main, polygamous) became monogamous in the Christian South, but not in the Islamic North, where a typical Muslim could marry as many as four wives. At any rate, those natives who were not converted to either of the two alien religions continued to practice polygamy, in spite of its condemnation by the church and the British colonial agents and agencies. In fact, some of the Nigerian civil servants who had more than one wife would present one of the wives as the official one to the government, while privately maintaining the rest in their villages. This is why it appears that the legal offense of bigamy is nonexistent in Nigeria, and laws against bigamy are impossible to enforce in Nigeria.

Nevertheless, where Christianity failed to undo the polygamous system, the economic structure has succeeded. For as more Nigerians got educated, they began to embrace Western economic systems. They were no longer satisfied with the low living standards their ancestors enjoyed, which depended on subsistence farming and petty trading. So they now engage in mechanized agriculture, commerce and industry, and even e-trade in modern times. Whereas their ancestors depended on storytelling sessions during moonlit nights for entertainment, the postindependence Nigerians got theirs from color TV shows. Today one sees satellite dishes mounted in every village to bring in CNN and other cable networks from the United States, Asia, and European countries. To maintain such a lifestyle meant that marriage, much less polygamy, was not a priority to those who wanted to enjoy first the good things that modern life could offer to them. Furthermore, it is well known that highly educated people, whether in Nigeria or elsewhere, tend to have fewer children than their less-educated forebears.

However, the pursuit of material wealth to support the kind of modern life that some contemporary, educated Nigerians hanker after, often causes degeneration of their moral stature. Such factors as the urbanization of former rural communities in Nigeria, Western education that often takes one away from one's village, Christianity, and the acquisition of foreign cultures have all combined to confuse and divert unwary modern Nigerians from the moral values of their primordial societies, which Christianity and foreign social scientists characterized variously as heathen, pagan, or savage, and their culture as superstitious, demonic, and archaic. Besides, some of the modern Nigerians believe that the constant village elders' reminder that all their citizens were descendants of common ancestors—for that reason, they were a family—was no longer applicable to them. They think that in the big towns and cities, the indigenous gods and goddesses and their priests and priestesses were no longer there to admonish or chastise them against committing immoral and unethical behaviors. In fact, some Christians and educated Nigerians sometimes consider their ancestors, godhead, and other spirit beings dead.

No matter what their preferred religion or ideology, most Nigerian immigrants who received good home training and moral education from their parents have continued to use them as useful tools to modify their behavior so as to avoid committing crimes and offenses that could take them to jail or earn them one form of punishment or another. They seem to exercise good moral judgment in everything they do in spite of the pressures of the so-called modern life.

NIGERIAN AMERICAN FAMILY LIFE AND VALUES

The changes that have taken place in Nigerian families and traditional institutions paved the way for the new family values of Nigerians in the United States. However, it should be noted that, in the main, their family values are still predicated upon their premigration religious and ethical morality, as well as on their folk beliefs and worldview. Some of them still believe, as they did in Nigeria before coming to the United States, that humans are at the center of all creations, yet they understand that being at that center involves maintaining a good relationship with other creations in the universe. It is an understanding that emanates from a metaphysical or cosmological belief in otherness: one that causes a person to seek to treat other creations in the universe and fellow human beings with respect, regardless of their ethnic, racial, national, and religious extractions. Above all, those Nigerians raised in the village are careful in taking any actions that could be deemed offensive to their dead-living ancestors and other spirit beings, because even when such offensive acts are not politically and legally actionable, they could be by the law of karma, or the law of natural retribution. They dare not rush in where angels fear to tread, as it were.

Furthermore, to ensure that they maintain order in the universe, Nigerian families affiliate themselves with religious organizations, such as the church, the mosque, and, quite recently, the temple, or with mystical and esoteric organizations like the Rosicrucians and the Masons. However, some cults have been exploiting the religious and mystical fervor of unwary Nigerians by

Worshipers at the Christ Apostolic Church of America, Inc., Jamaica, New York. Courtesy of the church.

Ethnic church. Courtesy of the author.

converting them into members of secret societies that destroy or cause harm to their fellow human beings. The more popular esoteric organizations that Nigerians are attracted to when they arrive in this country are the Rosicrucian Order and the Grail Message, and the Christian organizations they join include Full Gospel, God's Endtime Army, Campus Crusade for Christ, Inter-varsity Christian Fellowship, and the Navigators. Besides joining such international Christian organizations, Nigerian Americans have joined hands with other Africans to found the African Christian Fellowship here in the United States, as well as opening branches of the first indigenous African Pentecostal Church, the Eternal Sacred Order of Cherubim and Seraphim, in major cities. That church, which was founded in 1925 by the Baba Aladura, Moses Orimolade Tunolase, has since established its branches also in many West African countries and London, drawing most of its membership from Nigerian and African immigrants in those countries. The Aladuras (as they are called by Nigerian writers) combine Christian rituals and indigenous African religious rites in their church worship and celebrations.

THE BASIS OF NIGERIAN AMERICAN FAMILY VALUES

Having touched on what causes Nigerian Americans to form their new family values, the next thing for us to do is to answer the question, "What constitutes their family values?" While it is difficult to determine what constitutes the values that each individual family treasures, we can at least point out the very constituents of the values commonly shared by Nigerians as a group. That means we are dealing with group characteristics that include strong family ties, religious morality, hard work and diligence, respect for otherness, and ethnic primacy.

Strong Family Ties

Strong family ties are the foundation upon which Nigerian family values are built, wherever the families may be. This is so because Nigerians place a lot of emphasis on the continuity of the family name. As a patriarchal society, sons are trained to be strong and assertive and to develop leadership qualities that will enable them to inherit the leadership roles of their fathers at home, should such fathers die or become old, ill, or infirm. They are supposed to be providers of their family members' needs and to give them security as well as emotional and economic protection at all times. Also, the sons are trained to make sacrifices (including giving up their lives, if need be) that ensure the survival of the family and its good name—*Aha m efula* in Igbo.

From time to time, men have left their wives and children in Nigerian villages for big towns and cities in search of jobs that would earn them the money they could send home for the upkeep of all their people, who include members of the nuclear and extended families. In the United States, Nigerian immigrants do the same. They leave their families in one American city to go elsewhere for the purpose of working to make money for the upkeep of their family members both in the United States and in Nigeria. Also, because Nigerian immigration in the United States is a relatively new phenomenon, each Nigerian American is still able to retain his home in Nigeria, especially now that they are allowed by law to enjoy dual citizenship.

Some of the Nigerian American men find themselves in trouble if they married American women who do not understand their husbands' family obligations, which they must carry out as a necessary aspect of their family values. Nigerian parents who envisage the trouble do strongly admonish their sons even before they emigrate from Nigeria for the United States to avoid marrying American women. On the other hand, American girlfriends of such Nigerians do not understand why their men are afraid to propose marriage even when it is very obvious that they are both in love. The answer lies in the fact that Nigerian marriage is not a contract between a man and a woman in love. Rather, it is a pact between families of the two prospective spouses. Even if the American family sanctions the marriage, the Nigerian prospective husband cannot go ahead and marry without express permission of his parents back home in Nigeria. To date, marriages between Nigerian and American spouses without prior Nigerian parental approval are rare. But those Nigerians who are genuinely in love with American partners have always visited Nigeria with such partners for their parents' approval and blessing before they marry.

Finally, Nigerian men are afraid of being divorced by their spouses. They fear that they would be ridiculed back home in Nigeria because they are not able to *control* their spouses. That fear is real to them because the U.S. family law in almost every case gives the custody of young children to their mothers. Second, children of divorce always lose out on the guidance, control, and training of their fathers. In the end, the strict sexual rules and behavior of the Nigerian families are compromised, because the divorced women have sexual freedom. Men who were not able to accept their new marital status have sometimes killed their spouses and themselves, abandoned their children, and returned to Nigeria, or relocated to other American cities.

Their situation would be different in Nigeria, where, if the threat of divorce was discovered in a family, the parents of the two spouses, the church, and members of the extended families, as well as other cultural organizations, would do everything they could to mediate, counsel, and help in any way possible to reconcile the spouses so as to head off the prospective divorce. Once Nigerian Americans have filed for divorce, many factors work against other Nigerians taking actions to prevent the pending divorce: actions similar to the mediation efforts that prove quite successful in Nigeria. Sometimes, however, cases of nonlegal mediation efforts of Nigerians have been very successful, but those cases are rare. For their children's well-being, many Nigerian American men have adjusted their roles in their families to allow their wives to have their way if they wanted to take a leadership role in their family.

Religious Morality

The moral behavior of Nigerian Americans is influenced by their deep religious beliefs and worldview. Whether they were raised in the church, the mosque, or in any of their indigenous religions, it would be extremely unusual for a Nigerian to be an atheist. For that reason, they strive to live according to the Ten Commandments of the Bible or the preaching from the Qur'an. And, above all, they are constantly reminded of the consequences of such "unrighteous" acts as incest, greed, hypocrisy, adultery, fornication, and covetousness, which are considered abominable in their indigenous religions. Such acts are punishable by the omniscient, omnipresent, and omnipotent dead-living ancestors. In other words, that fear of the dead-living ancestors' punishment is one of the reasons why they strive to do things that are morally and ethically acceptable to their people and society at large. If they do wrong things, they are the first to apologize for their wrongdoings, but if they think what they have done is morally and ethically correct, they cannot apologize for it, even if their action is politically and, in some cases, legally incorrect. They fear the reprisals of their ancestors, gods and goddesses, and other spirit beings more than those of fellow human beings. This is why some Americans think that Nigerian Americans are arrogant and proud.

As has been discussed, many Nigerians belong to one religious organization or another, which ensures that the sermons they hear from the church, mosque, or temple will continue to guide them as they strive to lead good moral lives. This is especially so with the older generation of Nigerians, and they rarely get into trouble with the law. But the younger generations—those born after the Nigerian civil war, when churches were no longer in charge of schools, and those born in the United States, where parents do not have as much control of their children as those in Nigeria—are more likely to commit crimes that bring shame to their families and to other Nigerians at home and abroad.

Hard Work and Diligence

Because over 60 percent of Nigerian population live in rural areas, their economy is agro-based, but it is one that is not mechanized. The farmers, as we have already seen, are subsistence farmers and petty traders. They go to work from sunrise to sunset. Even the children who attend schools are asked to join their parents to work on the farmlands after school. By the time they graduate from Nigerian high schools and attend college in the United States, they would have learned to work very hard.

Furthermore, when they arrive in their new land, they are motivated by the concept of the American dream to work even harder. They do so with the belief that the harder they work (and doing so very diligently), the more they reap the rewards of their hard work and diligence. For doing so can enable them to buy cars, pay their bills, save enough money for everything they need, and still leave some to send to their people back home in Nigeria.

Above all, their success rate at school is second to none because they are used to working hard in Nigeria in poor weather and under less-favorable economic and social conditions. In fact, coming to the United States, where technology has simplified many things, including calculators to solve math problems and TV monitors and projectors to study science subjects, makes American education seem easy for the immigrants. In addition, they study in air-conditioned classrooms, offices, and libraries. So they take advantage of a more conducive atmosphere in which to study and learn. Besides, they could work to support themselves and their families while still in college, which is a privilege that is not easily tenable in Nigeria.

Another factor that motivates Nigerian immigrants to work hard and diligently is the competition that is built into the Nigerian age-grade system. An age-grade is a group of children born within a period of three years. As a part of their socialization process, they are trained to work hard to imbibe their indigenous culture and customs. Boys especially are officially named in an open ceremony when the individual members of the group attain ages sixteen through eighteen. During the official outing, members of the age-grade are expected to perform the same physical and mental tasks without failure. Anyone who fails to perform well is dropped out of the group, and that becomes a big disgrace to his individual family, compound, or village. Before they come of age, they already are exposed to such manly activities as wrestling matches, war games, and sporting activities that task their individual prowess and physical endurance—a necessary rite of passage.

Once the age-grade has performed well, they are given a name, and only then are they allowed to marry as legal adults. Their outing ceremony is comparable to the commencement exercises of American universities and colleges, full of pomp and pageantry.

This indigenous rite of passage mirrors a part of the British-oriented university exercise in contemporary Nigeria, where a class of admitted university students must graduate from college after four years. If any of them fails to graduate with the rest, he or she is asked to withdraw from school, which is to say that the failing ones do also *graduate* into obscurity and disgrace. This is why only the tough ones attend colleges in Nigeria. But that idea of age-grade motif is not lost to Nigerian immigrants in the United States, who must of necessity report their achievements to their people, family, and village through letters, telephone conversations, and e-mail, or messages sent through those visiting Nigeria. The graduates and achievers themselves may do so in person, and come back to the United States and continue working hard toward greater achievements. You can hear villagers describing the nonachieving Nigerian immigrants in the United States as lost sheep of their villages, because such persons rarely visit home or send money for improvement projects of their original homes, villages, and clans.

So, in order to ensure that they are not regarded as nonachievers or failures, Nigerian immigrants would do any job, however menial, to make money that helps them to achieve whatever goals they have set for themselves. The American idea of the dignity of labor encourages them to serve as janitors, taxi drivers, dishwashers, farm laborers, and night watchmen in spite of their college degrees, until their graduate work is over or they get more befiting and better-paying jobs. Even those of them who do the menial jobs are highly regarded in Nigeria, if they are able to send money regularly to their people, train some of their siblings in school, or build some relatively good houses for their families in Nigeria.

Respect for Otherness

Otherness is the condition of one being perceived as strange or different from other people or groups. As a result of having been raised in a pluralistic society that practices both monotheism and polytheism, as well as monogamy and polygamy, older Nigerian immigrants have respect for otherness. They know that they are in some ways different from other Americans, but that does not make them feel superior or inferior. That is why, in the beginning of their immigration journey, they were not affected psychologically by race or ethnicity to the degree that other racial or ethnic minorities in the United States were. They were that way because, unlike other new American immigrants, they believed that they were here mainly for the achievement of their desire to work hard so as to enjoy better economic, social, and educational opportunities. They did not sincerely believe that they were part of the American society, only short-term or long-term visitors. For that reason, if racism or ethnic bigotry affected them to a point where they could no longer achieve the purpose for which they came to the United States, they would voluntarily return to their people in Nigeria and continue life from where they left off. This attitude explains in part why many of them were not interested in politics, but were prepared to take up any honest job that paid them money. Ironically, however, that attitude has since changed radically as a result of the sordid life that Nigerians at home are subjected to everyday. And the more the immigrants visit Nigeria, the more they confront the poor sociopolitical and economic mismanagement of the ruling elite, which not too many people are eager to return to. So, in the end, Nigerians have begun seriously to adjust themselves emotionally and psychologically to accept the United States as their permanent home, and to see other Americans as their new and permanent neighbors.

Ethnic Primacy

Ethnic primacy is a deeply cherished Nigerian family value. Sometimes people mistake it for ethnic supremacy, which assumes a position of superiority or authority over all other ethnic or racial groups. On the contrary, ethnic primacy is the idea that the ethnic group is superior to any individuals, families, villages, or towns within the ethnic group, in terms of position or authority. It is that idea that causes people to serve and sacrifice whatever they can to sustain the survival of their people, whether here in the United States or back home in native Nigeria. That is why during the precolonial times, individual ethnic peoples of Nigeria could raise armies of fighting men not only to fight intertribal wars in defense of their people without pay; the soldiers would also do the same if they were asked to fight to acquire other tribal people's lands in order to expand their own. In modern Nigeria, the Biafran leader, General Emeka Odumegwu-Ojukwu, not only risked his personal safety and that of his family to fight Nigerians who killed, maimed, and raped the Igbo people in Northern Nigeria but he also used millions of dollars he inherited from his millionaire father to wage the Nigeria-Biafra War on behalf of his Igbo people. Although Easterners lost the war, the Igbo won the battle of ethnic cleansing and ethnic pride Nigeria waged against them. Some of them, who fought the war, drew strength and courage from Odumegwu-Ojukwu's personal sacrifices.

In the United States, Nigerian immigrants do everything to shelter, clothe, and feed newly arrived Nigerians until they get settled. Instead of allowing their fellow Nigerians or ethnic peoples to go on welfare, they would rather share with them whatever they have in their family without asking for any reward in future. The practice is a part of the demands of their highly extolled extended-family system.

The downside to this family value is that when mismanaged, it can result in ethnic bigotry and lack of patriotism. In fact, since after the Nigeria-Biafra War, Nigeria has found it difficult to produce a true political leader. So far, the ruling military and civilian political leaders have allowed ethnic primacy to degenerate into ethnic supremacy. For that reason, instead of Nigerians finding a way to nurture true nationalism, they talk about but do not carry out conducting conferences of sovereign nations within the Nigerian nation. And in the United States, Nigerian immigrants have not shown as much love for their native country as they have done for their individual ethnic peoples. Perhaps that is why they have not been able to develop any plans that could help solve some of Nigeria's sociopolitical and economic problems the way that Jewish Americans, Polish Americans, and Irish Americans have been doing in Israel, Poland, and Ireland. Yes, the Igbo people in the United States used their sense of ethnic primacy to help end the Nigeria-Biafra War and to help the survivors of the war to start life anew. But the question remains, "When can Nigerian Americans transcend their ethnic primacy so as to embrace national primacy as a valued family value in their new country or native land ?"

MAINTAINING NIGERIAN AMERICAN FAMILY VALUES

The children of any family acquire their values through socialization. In the socialization process, individuals acquire the values, attitudes, beliefs, and perceptions of their culture or subculture, including religion, nationality and social class. "Generally, the child conforms to the parents' expectations in acquiring an understanding of the world and its people. Being impressionable and knowing of no alternative conceptions of the world, the child accepts these concepts without questioning" (Parrillo 1998, 563). So the Nigerian American family values outlined previously are learned and maintained through parents, ethnic associations, folkways, and religion and by developing positive attitudes toward education.

The Role of Parents

The family values that children acquire and cherish are greatly determined by the roles they observe their parents play daily. This is so because children's first social experiences are those they acquire in the microcosmic society of the family home. If they see their father loving their mother passionately and caring for the children themselves, they grow up to love and respect women and children in their adult life. The same applies to the mother and children of both sexes. If, on the other hand, the children observe their parents fighting all the time, expressing all forms of unwholesome behavior, they will imbibe and express such behaviors later in life, unless there have been some better and more positive behaviors inculcated in them between their early childhood and adulthood.

Also, parents who get up early to work hard and diligently create a peaceful and loving home environment and spend some good quality time with their children, as well as convey messages of love of their particular god and fellow humans, peaceful coexistence with people of different ethnic, racial, economic, and gender groups, and love of one's country in word and in deed, do serve as true role models for their children. Some of these roles and messages are not easily understood or apprehended by Nigerian American children because the larger society sends out mixed and subliminal messages to them. It uses media that are more advanced and sophisticated than those their parents acquired in their native Nigeria: television shows, peer groups in school, and other external forces that American children in general are exposed to. All that makes it harder for parents to control their children the way they would have done back home in Nigeria. Above all, some state and family laws are making it very difficult for Nigerian American parents to take control of their wayward children.

The Role of Nigerian Ethnic Associations

The Nigerian ethnic associations in the United States have the primary purpose of offering a comfort zone to all their present and future members. As immigrants arrive in the country, they are given some temporary accommodation until they are able to find a permanent one. They are given as much information as is necessary for them to absorb the cultural shock that every newcomer is confronted with and the guidance they need for working toward the achievement of the aims of their immigration to the United States. Once they have found their feet and become the new Americans, the purpose of the ethnic associations takes a different tone: to promote the distinct ethnic characteristics of their indigenous Nigerian cultures, especially those that add to the resourcefulness of the vibrant American sociocultural life.

In addition, the ethnic associations are organs of social control of their members. They intervene in domestic quarrels of their married members, grant some loans to members who are facing eviction from their apartments because they are unable to pay their rents, give moral and ethical admonitions during cultural meetings, and contribute money for sociopolitical developments of their people at home in Nigeria. Above all, the elders of the ethnic associations are culturally bound to represent here the Nigerian parents and ancestors back there in Nigeria. That means that although members are not legally bound to obey the admonitions, the elders know that they could be found in default of their cultural duties if they failed to admonish the young people against any behavior that could land them in jail or earn them expulsion from their ethnic associations. On the other hand, younger members of the associations are equally obligated to politely warn their elders against committing social and criminal offenses that could bring shame and disgrace not only the to offenders themselves but also to Nigerian Americans and their native Nigeria.

In essence, the work the associations do complements and fosters the efforts that individual Nigerian American families are making to inculcate family values in their children. That is why such mottoes and apothegms as "Unity is strength," "Be your brother's keeper," "Pride goeth before a fall," and "Cut your coat according to your size," are adopted as guiding principles of the ethnic associations. They echo the ethnic morality and ethos encouraged in Nigeria.

The Role of Education

Many Nigerian immigrants come to the United States to acquire Western education. However, the type of education they received in Nigeria was a mixture of Western education (offered formally in the classrooms) and traditional education (offered informally at home). The former type requires use of books and trained teachers, but the latter involves listening to oral instructions and the guidance of elders, a method of learning best offered during storytelling sessions. Parental involvement as well as adult role models are active and necessary participants in that system of education.

However, many parents do not have or make enough time to teach their children at home. Some of them do not hold well-paying jobs. For that reason, they would prefer to work at a second job to make enough money for the upkeep of their families here in the United States and their people in Nigeria. Furthermore, some of the parents do not have enough knowledge of science and technology to enable them to teach their children at home. Also, most educated Nigerians do not learn to type, so when they come to the United States, they are not able to help themselves or their children learn or do anything with the computer. To hide their inadequacy in this regard, they may manufacture all kinds of subterfuge, including not having the time, to avoid teaching their children.

Still, parents have always found a way to teach their children at home, by hiring tutors or sending their children to centers where they are taught how to take SAT and GRE tests. The parents may enroll in computer classes, which ultimately enables them to use computers to teach their children. In the end, such parents also use the computer for their own professional advancement and research.

EMBRACING THE EMERGING CULTURE

The sociocultural ambiance of the United States compels Nigerian immigrants to drop some of their Nigerian culture so as to make room for the more appropriate cultural aspects of the United States. On the other hand, some of the positive aspects of the Nigerian culture they brought to the United States have helped to improve some aspects of the American culture wherever some improvement or modification was in order. The give-and-take nature of cultural adaptation, which is necessary in every socialization process, happens because cultures have always been clashing with or invading each other since the beginning of civil societies. But, in the end, the positive results of such invasions are that both the winning and losing cultures learn from each other, which is a process through which cultures are merged. We see this nature of cultural invasions in such powerful societies as Great Britain and the United States, which have borrowed so much from the Egyptian, Babylonian, Greek, and Roman civilizations. Hence, we find that the surviving superpower, the

United States, is such because of the aggregation of positive cultural elements of the immigrants (including Nigerians) who come from every corner and clime of the earth.

Family Structure

To fit well in their new country, Nigerian Americans have to conform to the idea of belonging to monogamous families. A man or woman who has more than one spouse at a time could be arrested and jailed for committing bigamy in the United States, a social crime that is recognized but not easily prosecuted in Nigerian courts of law. Also, the economic system, worldviews, and cosmological beliefs that directly or indirectly promote polygamy in Nigeria are irrelevant to the American society. For example, all children born in the United States, regardless of their gender, typically are regarded with

Ethnic church wedding.

equal love, unlike in traditional Nigerian societies where male children seem to count for more than female children. And, even though men could father children out of wedlock there and have no financial or emotional investment in such children, in the United States, if a man fathers a child within or outside of wedlock, he must pay for the child's financial support. Those who fail to support their children financially at least can be arrested and prosecuted in court as deadbeat fathers. In essence, family laws in the United States restrict the family structure from polygamy to monogamy and demand financial and emotional support of children born to married or unmarried parents.

Religion

Because the Nigerian immigrants attended mission or government schools in which Bible knowledge was taught as part of Western education in Nigeria, most of them are Christians. The few Muslims who came continued to worship in the mosques, but the changes in their social, educational, and economic life and worldview caused some of them to convert to Christianity. Such Muslims recognize the fact that the law does not allow them to marry more than one wife, and those who desperately need to get a green card through the marriage of American spouses may find such spouses from among members of other organized religions that promote monogamy. Furthermore, there are no priests and priestesses or gods and goddesses and their shrines that could enable the worshippers of indigenous Nigerian religions to continue in their faiths here in the United States. Like some of the Muslims, they are forced by the new social order to convert to Christianity. The only denominations of Christianity that continue to practice their faith in African churches without any significant structural changes are the Pentecostals, such as the Eternal Sacred Order of Cherubim and Seraphim and the Celestial Church of Christ. Nevertheless, although they permit members of their church to practice polygamy in Nigeria, their members cannot do so in the United States. But in order to accommodate the changes that are taking place in all aspects of their immigrant life, members of those African churches are gradually changing their African musical instruments into more sophisticated American ones; and their worship, which was originally conducted mostly in Nigerian indigenous languages, is now conducted mainly in English.

Associations

Although the associations that Nigerian immigrants subscribe to when they arrive in the country are mainly ethnic, the wider educational, professional, religious, and social groups to which they are affiliated demand that they seek membership in other kinds of associations, such as national and regional associations, alumni associations, student organizations, professional and business organizations, political organizations, and cultural groups. Each of these organizations broadens their educational, cultural, and professional perspectives beyond those they acquired through belonging only to ethnic associations. Considering, therefore, their enormous importance to the new immigrants, these organizations will be discussed at length in Chapter 4; suffice it to say here that they are the more practical and potent means of Americanizing the Nigerian immigrants as soon as they arrive in this country.

Other Social Institutions

There is no gainsaying that Nigeria and the United States are two structurally different societies. As such, the Nigerian immigrants have to change their notions of social institutions so as to embrace the American ones. Already, we have seen what changes they have made in marriage and family structure, in religion, and in ethnic associations. However, in order for them to adjust fully their new sociocultural lives, the Nigerian Americans must also be prepared to drop their premigration baggage in areas of gender equality, ethnic equality, and socioeconomic equality.

As a patriarchal society, Nigeria promotes directly and indirectly the notion of domination of women by men. It is a practice that is very visible in their military, civil service, and universities. Being products of such a society, Nigerian immigrants come with the idea that men should count for more than women. So Nigerian men have to accept the fact that all humans are created equal. That includes allowing their spouses and female children to receive education that is equal to that of males. Also, following such education, women should be able to get into the workforce that men had claimed in the past as their birthright.

Furthermore, as the ethnic peoples of Nigeria acquired Western education and values, they lost some of their cosmological beliefs, including respect for otherness. As a result, the dominant ethnic groups such as the Hausa, the Igbo, and the Yoruba began to claim superiority over other ethnic groups whom they dominated because of their small populations. One sees the domination in Nigerian government appointments and social amenities. Unfortunately, some Nigerian immigrants from those dominant groups who have imbibed the undue superior self-esteem do come to the United States with it. But when they arrive in a society that has its own injustices and prejudices, they are humbled in that they become double minorities: black and foreign. In fact, some of their fellow black people, African Americans, treat them as foreigners even when such Nigerians have become citizens through naturalization. In a word, the new social order forces them to modify their behavior and to crave ethnic and gender equality as well as racial harmony.

Also, as a highly stratified society, Nigeria knowingly and unknowingly promotes discrimination among various socioeconomic classes. The military men lord it over civilians, professors over administrative workers, government workers over businesspeople, and of course, every other set of workers treats farmers with some measure of condescension. At any rate, when the Nigerian immigrants come, they find to their utter dismay that neither high education nor public or private employment confers on them the kind of respect or acknowledgment it would have in Nigeria. Because of the American notion of the dignity of labor, although citizens may be as obsessed with social class and ranking as in Nigeria, their primary worry is first the ability to work and maintain themselves and their families financially. Besides, anyone can become a celebrity through personal achievements in their chosen career, which enables them to join the elite. In fact, one of the most celebrated individuals in the United States, Bill Gates, could have been a laughingstock in Nigeria for being a college dropout, despite his immeasurable wealth in the computer business. In other words, Nigerian immigrants have learned that socioeconomic class is a fluid and transient classification in the United States, where the ideas of individual opportunity, dignity of labor, and the American dream can, and often do, encourage people to work hard to become whatever they dream of becoming, including becoming the president.

Dropping their premigration cultural baggage has made it possible for Nigerian Americans to adjust their behavior so as to adapt to all areas of American national life. Such adjustment affirms the American belief "that all men are created equal, that they are endowed by their Creator with certain unalienable Rights, that among these are Life, Liberty and the pursuit of Happiness." These are rights that no Nigerian enjoys at home, hence their leaving Nigeria for the United States. How well the Nigerian immigrants have utilized the available opportunities to enable them to adapt fully and meaningfully to the new social order is the subject of the remaining chapters of this book.

4

Educational and Economic Adjustment

In Chapter 2, our exploration of the causes of Nigerian immigration in the United States revealed that the quest for Western education was a dominant motivation. In fact, coming to the United States made it possible for many qualified Nigerians, who could not have been admitted into the few colleges and universities in their country (due to limited facilities and trained manpower), to begin their education with better facilities and well-trained professors. Upon graduation, some of the students returned to Nigeria, while others decided to stay in the United States as immigrants. It is thus important to know how this group of new immigrants have fared, in terms of getting the quality education they craved, and whether they have achieved their American dream.

This chapter explores Nigerian Americans' educational adjustment and how it has affected for good their consequent occupational and economic adjustment and development. That exploration begins with a careful examination of this new group of immigrants' educational trends, employment, and income.

EDUCATIONAL TRENDS

Nigerian Americans' educational trends began with their quest for formal Western education, which started from precolonial through colonial to postcolonial periods in Nigeria, until they came to the United States and became immigrants. Each phase of their journey had a profound effect on the type of education they received, which ultimately determined their economic status in particular times and places in their lives.

From Traditional to Western Education

The traditional education, which Nigerians practiced before the coming of whites into their societies, promoted a lot of oral performance in literature, philosophy, religion, indigenous technology, and fine arts and crafts at the expense of pure science and technology. The elders of each community and parents of each family engaged in an oral tradition in which children were told stories of the founding of their land and the mythology and legends of their ethnic peoples and were taught the poetry and songs of yesteryears during storytelling sessions. The priestly caste divined the wills of the gods and goddesses, offered sacrifices to them, and presided over religious rituals and celebrations. The fine artists taught young people how to carve various religious icons, talking drums, and calabash wares. Female elders taught young women how to weave straw mats and hats, make earthenware and pottery with terra-cotta, and draw artistic patterns on their mud-and-wattle houses. Also, they engaged in facial scarifications and body makeup with chalk and special cosmetic liquids (*uli* in Igbo). Furthermore, men taught boys war and ritual dances, and women taught girls bridal and general entertainment dances.

In all these, ethnic worldviews and folklore were handed down from fathers to sons, and from sons to grandsons. Women carried out the same oral tradition with their daughters and granddaughters. In a word, the philosophies of life and living were taught to the younger generations, who internalized them and, out of memory, handed down the same folklore to many generations of Nigerians after them.

Besides ordinary arts and crafts, Nigerians had their own indigenous technology. They produced war implements such as bows and arrows, machetes, guns, spears, firearms, and explosives (*nkunala*), with which they fought intertribal wars. Later in history, they used improved models of those implements to fight against the Arabs and Portuguese during the era of slave trade. And when in the late 1800s the British attempted to colonize their territories, Nigerians used the arms and weapons they had developed over the years to defend their territories until they were finally overrun in 1906. In essence, the education the people received was oral and was taught practically to the young by their elders from one generation to another.

Adaptation of Western Education

Once they conquered Nigeria, the British introduced their own system of education. However, their educators were only interested in teaching Nigerians the three R's—Reading, Writing, and Arithmetic—which helped them to raise some local labor force that could teach the Bible and conduct Sunday schools for white missionaries, to serve as interpreters and messengers in the British courts in Nigeria, and to train civil servants that propagated British colonial government and political systems in the country. The British were less interested in teaching the science and technology that would have helped Nigerians to develop their own industries and businesses. Instead, they encouraged nonmechanized agricultural systems that produced palm oil and kernel, corn, peanut, cocoa, and other cash crops that British agents in Nigeria shipped to their country for sustaining their industries. When the raw materials produced in Nigeria were turned into manufactured goods, British companies sold them to Nigerians at exorbitant prices. In a word, the Western education that the British propagated made Nigeria a consumer, instead of a producing, nation.

However, what Nigerians lost by not engaging fully in science and technology education was gained in literary studies, fine arts, and social sciences. For they turned their penchant for storytelling habits and music into a strong literary desire that turned their oral history, literature, religious practices, and worldviews into a written tradition later in their history. The effort Nigerians made in this aspect of their educational development was so successful that they are currently well-known for their written literature, which constitutes over 65 percent of what is known in the literary world as "African literature today."

Consequently, the first crop of Nigerian immigrants to receive gainful employment in the United States were graduates of the educational system that we have just described previously. Many of them were employed in the departments of English, History, Sociology, Psychology, and History of Arts, and some of them helped to develop the African, Africana, Black, or Ethnic Studies programs all over the United States, beginning from the 1960s. In fact, the books some of them wrote were used as foundation texts for Africana studies.

Adaptation of American Education

Educated Nigerian Americans are fully aware that they became immigrants principally because of the liberal education they first received in Nigeria. But they also know at firsthand the limitations of that education, which was pro-arts and oriented toward government employment. Therefore, in order to break free from the limitations of such education, many of the immigrants set aside the arts degrees they acquired in Nigeria and began working on other degree programs that would not only land them better paying jobs but would also make them seek employment outside of government departments and institutions. Hence, one finds that although parents may be professors of English, they may want their children to pursue medicine, law, computer science, nursing, or any of the various branches of engineering. Fortunately for such parents, who are professors, some of their universities have programs that allow their children and spouses to pursue their chosen educational courses with tuition waivers. Depending on how well they do, such children usually graduate and find jobs that pay them better than what some of their parents are paid. Besides, the encouragement they receive and the financial assistance they get through their parents' jobs make it easier for such children to do well, sometimes better than their parents did. But that happens only if they follow the guidance of their parents and university authorities. Above all, the greatest assets that such children have are their parents (who serve as role models), a conducive learning environment (both at home and on campus), and the good study habits inculcated in them, all of which they need to succeed in college and in life after college.

In a word, American education offers students a variety of courses that meet their individual needs. Also, it is not primarily tailored toward government employment only as is often the case in Nigeria. Instead, students in American institutions can move from one academic discipline to another without minding how long it takes them to graduate, unlike in Nigeria where a class of students admitted in a given academic year are expected to leave campus after the official duration of their course programs with or without earning their degrees. These are some of the reasons why American education is regarded by many educators in the world as a more libertarian system.

Opportunities for Obtaining an Education in the United States

In Nigeria, students bear the costs of all of their educational programs, from preschool through high school to college. For that reason, only those whose parents can financially support them are likely to study up to the seventh grade, the beginning of their secondary school education, in which they are taught mathematics and science subjects. That is why those who cannot afford the cost of secondary school education may still receive its equivalent (through private tutorial services), which is financially cheaper but tailored toward the study of arts and social sciences. Students who receive that kind of education can use their diplomas to find low-paying jobs in elementary schools and the civil service. However, the more brilliant ones among them could take General Certificate in Education (GCE) exams (which are the equivalent of GED in the United States) and go on to take Joint Admissions and Matriculation

Board (JAMB) exams (the equivalent of SAT in the United States) for admission into the universities. Usually, most of this category of students would pursue nonscience subjects due to lack of adequate preparation in science and mathematics because of nonavailability of science textbooks, modern science labs, and well-trained teachers of mathematics and the sciences.

In contrast, however, Nigerian immigrants have wonderful opportunities here in the United States for educating their children to the highest level they are capable of reaching. Such opportunities include free education from preschool to high school, tutorial services, adequate college and university accommodations for qualified applicants, diversified degree and nondegree programs, and work-study for needy students, as well as modern facilities and well-trained instructors, all of which make it easy for committed and hardworking students to succeed in their academic pursuits.

Nigerian American medical school graduate being "red capped" in a ritual ceremony. Courtesy of the author.

Free Education. The free education available to all American children from preschool to high school relieves Nigerian American parents of the financial burden that they would have been required to carry if they and their children were in Nigeria. Instead, parents take the opportunity of the free education to save some money for their children's college education. Secondly, the free education enables the children to receive mathematics and science education in addition to liberal arts education. With that kind of rounded education, Nigerian American children, like other American children, are prepared to pursue any academic majors they are interested in when they enter college or the university.

Also, in addition to being free, American precollege education programs do hire and pay from public funds tutors who help weak students to overcome their weaknesses in certain subject areas so as to enable them to graduate with the better students. Nigerian students do not have the same opportunity because the public schools are poorly funded, and that means that providing extra tutorial services for weak students is out of the question. Nevertheless, the children of rich parents do enjoy the luxury of receiving tutorial services either in private schools or at home at personal costs to their parents. The difference in the two systems is that, while all American children have equal opportunity to pursue public education offered by their states and local governments, Nigerian children do not enjoy the same playing field when it comes to the funding of their education; and secondary school education, which we take for granted in this country, is a rare commodity in Nigeria. Just recently, in the year 2000, the Nigerian government began talking about making elementary school education free to all children under the name of Universal Basic Education (UBE). When fully implemented, the program will benefit (and perhaps increase the number of) students only in grade schools. That means that many of them would still not be able to attend high school under the aegis of state and local governments, as it is here in the United States.

Adequate Number of Colleges and Universities. Nigeria, whose population is about one half of the population of the United States, has under fifty universities, compared to about fifty thousand universities and colleges in the United States. The combined student populations of Ohio State University at Columbus, the University of Texas at Austin, and the University of California at Los Angeles are more than the combined student populations of all Nigerian universities. Because of the limited space for qualified students seeking admission into Nigerian universities, only the brightest ones are admitted each year, except those who are admitted through what the university administrators call supplementary admissions, which are not based strictly on merit. That is why the students who are not admitted into the home universities seek admission into foreign ones, especially in the United States, England, France, and Canada. In fact, there is no well-known American university or college in which one cannot find a good number of Nigerian students and professors. Also, the junior/community college systems are very attractive to Nigerian students, who may not have enough money to pay for a four-year college education at a stretch. With associate degrees from such colleges, the graduates can work to make the money they need to complete their full degree programs after some time out.

The opportunity is even greater for Nigerian Americans who can stay in school as long as they are able to, or drop out of school without the fear of violating immigration laws. Besides, Nigerian American students know the best schools to apply to for admissions or financial institutions, including federal and state governments, for loans and sponsorship. These are opportunities that are not available to foreign students. In other words, considering the number of public and private colleges and universities, as well as community/junior colleges, any Nigerian American student who wants to acquire a higher education can find, through research, institutions that will accommodate his or her academic needs and financial support.

Diversified Programs. Beginning from the community college level through the universities, American institutions of higher learning offer so many diversified programs that all aspirant students' interests are fully covered. This is because those in charge of curriculum development in each school try their best to develop new programs that satisfy the needs of contemporary American societies. Also, new personnel committees of academic departments and human resources in all institutions are constantly advertising locally, nationally, and internationally new positions for faculty and administrators who teach and direct their newly created departments and programs.

The new developments in American university educational systems make Americans leaders in world university systems, because they have transformed from offering parochial American courses in the early stages of their university systems to offering courses that derive from issues and events from all over the world. This development in turn draws scholars from all parts of the world.

Nigerian American parents are aware of the diversified course programs and the schools best known for their excellence in offering distinguished programs. Also, they know from their experience of social stratification in Nigeria that success in education is key to acquiring good careers in an advanced country like the United States. So they take time to discuss with their children the institutions that produce students who, upon graduation, attract respectable employers.

Whether or not Nigerian American children are able to study in the prestigious schools, one big advantage they have over their counterparts in Nigeria is that they have the privilege of attending college all year round without any interruptions. The situation is most appreciated by Nigerian American parents who come from that part of Nigeria once called Biafra during their civil war, because schools and colleges were closed during the three years the war raged. And after the war, the military regimes constantly shut down universities whenever students demonstrated against some military decrees or directives that the students thought were unhelpful and unfair to the people—a right that Americans enjoy without reprisals from their government. Even within the postmilitary period, beginning from May 29, 1999, there were too many strikes by Academic Staff Union of Universities (ASUU)—an association of Nigerian university professors—against the federal government of Nigeria, which tended to paralyze the Nigerian university education. In some years, the students were forced by the strikes to stay home for up to five months of an academic year. In such years, the universities engaged in social promotion of students from one class to another without teaching them the courses that should qualify them as real university graduates when they were finally awarded their diplomas. Such deplorable educational situations in their native land are one of the factors that motivate Nigerian Americans to sponsor the education of their kith and kin in the United States or in Nigeria, sometimes at the expense of their immediate family's comfort.

Opportunities for Work-Study. Many Nigerians who apply for graduate admissions into American universities also apply for work-study. In many cases, they are offered admissions with appointments to serve as teaching associates and teaching/research assistants while they study for their master's degrees, or as assistant instructors, if they have already earned a master's degree and are studying for a doctorate. Some of the appointees are given salaries as well as tuition waivers for their spouses and children who study in the same institutions. By the time they earn their degrees, such persons are enabled to find good jobs that help them to apply for green cards and, thereafter, citizenship, if they had green cards while they worked and studied.

Furthermore, Nigerian professors who came to the United States with H-1—alien of distinguished merit—visas on sabbatical leave for one year, have had the opportunity to renew their visas yearly until they applied for a change of status, provided that they were ready to resign their positions in their home universities and that their host universities and businesses were prepared to offer them jobs that could enable them to apply for immigrant visas.

The more distinguished one is in his or her filed of specialization, the more chances he or she has in changing immigration status, especially if that specialization is in areas that American citizens do not have enough of a local workforce. As we have already seen, Nigerians did well in African, Africana, and Black Studies programs in the 1960s and 1970s, when there were fewer Americans, black and white, who had expertise in those fields. Since the early 1980s, however, many Americans have become authorities in those areas, so fewer and fewer universities are hiring Nigerians in that field than they did before.

Some Nigerian immigrants who are in this immigration category took advantage of the work-study programs to branch off from arts and social science programs to study law, computer science, and paramedical and paralegal programs, which also offered some opportunities for work-study. The opportunities not only added diversity to the programs that Nigerians enrolled in but also laid the foundation for the sponsorship and diversification of the programs that the immigrants' children and spouses could undertake if they so chose. So far, Nigerians at home and in the United States have been enriched by the opportunities that the work-study programs have created for them, which are rare in their native Nigeria.

Modern Facilities and Trained Personnel. The greatest advantage American education has over the Nigerian system, which Nigerian Americans have come to enjoy, is the modern facilities and trained personnel found in every American university or college. Instructors use TV monitors, overhead projectors, and audio- and videotapes to instruct their students. Some classroom complexes are equipped with other state-of-the-art high-tech facilities. Besides the classrooms being so modernized, the libraries, student dormitory rooms and centers are all air-conditioned and computer-wired for students' use. In fact, by the time students come to college, they are already computer-literate because they have learned how to use a computer from their parents or at school.

Initially, Nigerian Americans (except those born in the United States) are overwhelmed by the use of the high-tech gadgets as educational tools. However, as we have seen previously, schools and colleges do make provisions for tutoring their computer-illiterate students. In addition, such students are encouraged to take private lessons or receive tutoring to facilitate their other academic requirements, such as typing their written assignments, using the Internet and search engines to do research, and doing computer-based assignments given by their professors.

Apart from the modern facilities, highly trained American personnel makes their education superior to that of Nigeria. In addition to hiring regular professors to teach courses in their areas of specialization, American colleges and universities make extra effort to hire guest speakers and consultants from the private sector (mainly from industries and businesses) to teach their students in regular classes, as well as in seminars, conferences, and colloquia. Also, renowned professors from other institutions of higher learning are invited occasionally to come lecture or teach students of the host universities for some handsome honoraria. Thus, the exchange of ideas from all walks of life makes American education a more resourceful system and its graduates more productive workers.

Finally, the educational institutions make good efforts to provide their students living with disabilities facilities such as wheelchairs and specially designed houses, dormitories, and classrooms, as well as guide dogs and human guides. The facilities are provided to the students in order to make it possible for all Americans to enjoy equal rights to public education, thus enabling each and every one of them to become a useful and employable citizen.

Most of these opportunities are not available in Nigeria. In fact, except for highly educated and rich people, persons with any form of disability in Nigeria are usually forgotten by society, as far as higher public education is concerned, and they are sometimes regarded as private burdens to their individual families. Put differently, the educational administrators unwittingly consider the extra assistance that should be given to persons living with disabilities as a loss to the able-bodied students in Nigeria.

The influence of the American educational system goes beyond its borders. Quite recently, American-educated Nigerians who are in charge of modern Nigerian educational administration have begun to make cases for the provision of some of the modern facilities they themselves enjoyed while they schooled in the United States. The effort their government is making in that direction is complemented by those made by foreign and local charitable organizations and by individual Nigerian Americans who donate books, typewriters, computers, TV monitors, and copier machines to schools and colleges in their former towns and institutions in Nigeria. However, two factors influence people against doing more for their relations and alma maters: cost of shipping and lack of trained personnel to service and repair the pieces of equipment when they break down—and they do break down very frequently as a result of the erratic supply of electricity in Nigeria.

In sum, living in the United States enables Nigerian immigrants to bring a lot of good changes to the Nigerian educational system, in spite of the setbacks noted previously. And it is those changes that continue to promote further Nigerian immigration to the United States. Thus, the educational adjustment that Nigerian Americans have been making have helped their kith and kin in the United States and in Nigeria, to the mutual benefits of both countries.

ECONOMIC ADJUSTMENT

As we saw in Chapter 2, the first wave of Nigerian immigrants came primarily for Western education that the United States offered in its institutions of higher learning. Among the immigrants were those who had already earned college degrees in Nigeria and elsewhere but came mainly for graduate studies. Both college and graduate student immigrants made Nigerians one of the highly educated new immigrant groups, who found jobs in the public sector, especially in the universities and colleges. Their employment in those institutions predetermined the kinds of employment and income adjustments they would make after graduating from college and graduate school with degrees up to the highest levels. No matter what levels of degrees they earned, their employment and income opportunities were usually more than what they would have been in Nigeria.

Employment Adjustment

Nigerian immigrants' adjustment to work in the United States is influenced by their achievements as graduates of colleges or universities. Depending on their visa status, they are able to work in nonprofessional, professional, high-tech, and self-established small business settings.

Nonprofessional Jobs. Except those whom American institutions admit directly from Nigeria for graduate studies with financial benefits, such as teaching associate, teaching/research assistant, and assistant instructor appointments, or recipients of Nigerian federal and state government scholarships, the immigrants usually seek nonprofessional jobs to augment the financial assistance they receive from their parents and relatives. Often, the jobs they do are those that many American citizens are not too eager to do, including night watchmen, janitors, farmhands, restaurant workers, and nurses aides and assistants. Indeed, many of these jobs are hard, and yet pay minimum wages. However, although such jobs may seem menial to university students, the Nigerian immigrants, who have embraced the American idea of dignity of labor, are usually happy to do them for a while in order to be able to support other efforts they make to earn their degrees from the universities. The nonprofessional jobs would be considered beneath their dignity in Nigeria.

As seen in Table 2.5, of the 7,746 Nigerian immigrants admitted by major occupation in the 1998 fiscal year, 294 were hired for administrative support, 79 for precision production, craft, and repair, 83 for operator, fabricator, and laborer, 65 for farming, forestry, and fishing, while 4,839 had no occupations or did not report them. In other words, out of the 7,746 admitted, 522 began with nonprofessional jobs and 4,839 had no occupation or did not report their occupation. These two categories of Nigerian immigrants are the ones who begin their lives in the United States with nonprofessional jobs until they are able through further studies to change that kind of job after graduating from college or university.

Professional Jobs. In the 1998 fiscal year, 1,286 Nigerian immigrants were admitted with offers of professional specialty and technical occupations, 180 with executive, administrative, and managerial positions, 432 with sales occupation, and 487 with occupation in the service profession. Overall, a total of 2,385 Nigerian immigrants began their lives in the United States as professionals. Depending on whether they were full-time workers, many of them changed jobs after graduating from university, but the adjustment occurred in terms of attracting higher positions, earnings, and remunerations, as well as change of companies and institutions, but not the professions themselves. However, some of these professionals would change their occupations if, while engaging in their original professional practice, wanted to pursue other course majors that gave them more job satisfaction. For example, a few accountants wanted to enroll in the evening programs of law schools while they worked as accountants; after earning their law degrees and passing their bar exams, they adjusted their original occupation in order to utilize their expertise in the two closely related professions.

Furthermore, other professionals had to abandon completely their original professions to pursue new and unrelated ones. This category of immigrants practiced the professions they studied in Nigerian universities until they came to the United States. Although they found their profession not very satisfying, they stuck to it because Nigerian universities did not offer programs that covered their original professional interests. But on arrival in the United States, they seized the opportunity to pick and choose from many professional course offerings those that they were originally interested in. For instance, those who studied computer science in Nigeria were taught mainly the theoretical aspects of it but not the practical due to lack of adequately trained personnel and modern facilities in the field. For that reason, their limited experience in that field did not quite qualify them to work as computer scientists. Instead, they worked in related fields, such as marketing, accounting, and business management. When, eventually, they came to the United States as immigrants, they pursued their original interest in computer science even as they worked part-time in non-computer-related professions. These are the people who would eventually adjust their professional occupation and work in high-tech industries and establishments.

High-Tech Jobs. The second wave of Nigerian immigrants and those born in the United States took advantage of the engineering and technical programs that American universities offered to empower themselves in seeking jobs in high-tech businesses and industries. Upon graduation from the universities, some of them sought and got jobs from companies like Motorola, Texas Instruments, and computer companies situated in the Silicon Valley, while others were hired by government agencies like NASA. In addition, some of the Nigerian Americans who distinguished themselves in their university education were recruited by various engineering and construction firms as aerospace engineers, civil engineers, computer programmers, architects, biostatisticians, and lab technicians. And quite recently, some have been engaged as pharmacologists and chemical engineers in industries where the use of high-tech equipment is crucial. Although Nigerian Americans have made some progress in this area of employment, they are yet to beat their Asian counterparts, who embraced this area of employment before them.

Self-Established Small Businesses. Late in their immigrant history, Nigerian Americans have begun to establish their own small businesses, instead of depending wholly on government and other corporate employment. But these questions arise, "Are they doing so in the spirit of the general American entrepreneurship?" or "Are they merely following the footsteps of other new American immigrants, such as the Korean, Taiwanese, or Pakistani self-employed businessmen and women?" To answer the questions involves the exploration of the causes and consequences of establishing minority small businesses in the United States.

From previous discussions, we saw that early Nigerian immigrants were relatively highly educated before coming to the United States, that English was their national language, and that they depended on government and educational institutions for employment when they first arrived in the United States. That first crop of immigrants were few in number, and the positions they sought and got were limited in number as well. However, the jobs most of them sought were either those that American citizens were not qualified for, or could not and did not want to do. In addition, as more and more Nigerians came, the jobs open to them became more and more scarce; hence they decided to find other ways of surviving economically. Self-established small businesses became an attractive alternative, even though it was difficult for many of them to find the wherewithal to establish their fancied businesses. Still, they tried.

Theoretically, the Nigerians decided to establish their own small businesses because they realized the disadvantages of being a minority immigrant group in the United States, they had the opportunity to establish businesses that were native to them, and they could mobilize the resources that could sustain the businesses they chose to establish.

Disadvantage Theory. Some of the Nigerian scholars and graduate students who came during the first wave of Nigerian immigration in the United States were employed by universities to develop African, Africana, or Black Studies programs in the United States. They easily bonded with African American students, faculty, and the black community because they helped to give them some realistic image of Africa as they taught its literature, history, art, and music, which were an effective means of expressing African culture and civilization. Their white university colleagues were equally excited to learn more about Africa and its peoples from those who gave them authentic, insiders' information about the "dark continent." In the end, Americans of different racial and ethnic backgrounds developed some curious interest in learning about the continent. So some of them went to Africa, which they considered another frontier to be experienced. On their return to the United States, they told stories and wrote books about Africa that opened the eyes of administrators of American universities and government agencies to see the need for creating and developing African studies in their universities as well as good foreign policies on Africa in the State Department. One such administrator, George C. Bond, director of the Institute of African Studies at Columbia University, New York, has written:

> There is every reason for us to know something about Africa and to understand its past and the way of life of its peoples. Africa is a rich continent that has for centuries provided the world with art, culture, labor, wealth, and natural resources. It has vast mineral deposits, fossil fuels, and commercial crops.
>
> But perhaps most important is the fact that fossil evidence indicates that human beings originated in Africa. The earliest traces of human beings and their tools are almost two million years old. Their descendants have migrated throughout the world. To be human is to be of African descent. (from Ogbaa 1995, 6–7)

The Peace Corps volunteers who served in various parts of Africa gave further credence to the kind of information enunciated in this passage regarding Africa as a region of the world worthy of American exploration.

Ironically, however, the more American citizens became authorities in African studies, the less need there was for hiring Nigerians to teach courses in that field of university curricular offerings. So, beginning from the second half of the 1980s, Nigerian American scholars and professors became somehow marginalized.

In other areas of employment, Nigerian immigrants were faced with loss and scarcity of jobs even in fields where they were highly qualified, due to affirmative action in the hiring practices of government and academic institutions. They were (and still are) considered double minorities (because they are black and foreign-born), so they could not be offered jobs set aside for African Americans, unless such jobs were first offered to and refused by them. Also, their foreign accent did not help the Nigerian immigrants as they looked for jobs, despite their impressive credentials. But the most disabling factor that makes them a minority group in the American workforce emanates from their educational background; that is, the Nigerian educational system that did not prepare them for the type of technology-driven jobs that predominate the American labor market. Their work ethic and their cultural experience are not enough to help them in competing favorably for jobs with native-born Americans.

Furthermore, considering their general minority status and its inherent disadvantages, even the employed Nigerian immigrants easily feel frustrated by such factors as lack of upward occupational mobility, lack of rapport with other workers, and sometimes, acceptance of low-paying jobs for which they are overqualified. Therefore, in order to fight the frustration they felt from time to time in both public and private labor market, and to enhance their earning capacity, the disaffected Nigerian immigrant workers made the decision to establish and run their own small businesses. In time, such businesses grew in size and importance, adding a significant Nigerian streak to the overall American industry and economy.

Resources Theory. Capitalism, the United States economic system, involves investment in and ownership of the means of production, distribution, and exchange of wealth made and maintained chiefly by private individuals and corporations. Hence for anyone to participate in the system, he or she should note that capital and labor are a *sine qua non* that they ought to have ready before engaging in any business establishment. Also, the prospective Nigerian immigrant entrepreneurs may have been strongly motivated by their minority status to achieve upward economic mobility and to save enough money as capital to start their business. Yet, without developing the capacity to effectively mobilize and use the necessary resources that constitute labor, they cannot succeed in creating and running a successful business. For Nigerian and other new immigrant groups in the United States, the resources necessary for immigrant entrepreneurship are class, ethnic, and family resources.

With regard to class resources, Nigerian business owners are in the main college educated, urban, and middle class. At college, they learn business management skills that help them eventually to manage their own businesses; after college, they find jobs that pay middle-class salaries, some of which they set aside as capital for setting up their prospective businesses; and they tend to site such businesses in urban areas where there are concentrations of ethnic and minority communities, who serve as the consumers of the goods and products from the Nigerian immigrants' businesses.

Those who buy the products (initially fellow Nigerian Americans) usually help to promote such businesses without charging any fees. They do so by giving oral and written information on the businesses to others during ethnic association meetings. In addition, university student associations patronize some of the entrepreneurs and their businesses during students' social and cultural events, such as homecoming, Black History Month, and commencement celebrations. For example, at Southern Connecticut State University in New Haven, the Multicultural Center, under the aegis of the Student Affairs unit of the university, promotes from time to time such events as the Taste of Africa, the Taste of Asia, and the Taste of the Caribbean, in which students from countries making up those demographic groups of the university exhibit their ethnic foods, handicraft, clothing, music, and dances to the university community and their neighbors.

Representatives of Nigerian American businesspeople usually take advantage of such occasions to advertise their products and goods. Through the ads, African Americans are able to place orders for Nigerian clothes and fabrics for the celebration of Black Christmas, also called Kwanza, which in turn promotes the dissemination of the general black culture and civilization in North America. In return, some of the immigrant entrepreneurs have been employing their ethnic students to work part-time in some of their businesses. In addition, they create the same opportunities for business majors to do summer jobs, or graduate students to receive their internship training at their businesses, from time to time.

Regarding family resources, the Nigerian parents and their young adults, as well as members of their extended families, are involved in various aspects of the management of the immigrant businesses. To begin with, small business owners do not establish their businesses upon arrival in the United States from Nigeria. They start thinking about doing so while they are holding jobs in private and public business institutions. And when eventually they start their own businesses, they develop a work schedule that allows them to continue working at their job places in the day while their spouses work at their own businesses also in the day, until they return to their self-established businesses in the evenings. Members of their extended families and young adult children take turns doing house chores while the spouses are away to work at their business stores, and their children attend school during the day. Uncles, aunts, cousins, and other relatives stay home to baby-sit children; they also cook and clean the house.

If such extended family members are young adults, they could be engaged as useful assistants in the running of such small family businesses as food service, janitorial jobs, beauty salons, and grocery stores, which do not require high levels of education and managerial skills. In most cases, the family members are not paid regular salaries; instead, they are given free meals, shelter, clothing, medical insurance, and other necessaries of life by the business owners.

Apart from the human resources that have been discussed, Nigerian business owners have been assisted over the years in establishing and expanding their businesses by the financial contributions of members of their class, ethnic peoples, and families. The contributions may take the forms of outright grants, loans from rotating credit accounts of their ethnic associations, and funds from business partners.

Unlike many other new American immigrants, most Nigerian Americans are still first-generation immigrants, which means that they still have parents and other members of their extended families to whom they can go for financial assistance in Nigeria. That includes getting outright grant of money they can use as capital to establish their small businesses. As seen in previous chapters, traditionally, the family (both nuclear and extended) is the basic social unit in the Nigerian culture. In consideration of that fact, rich members of one's family do not consider the financial contributions they make toward the establishment of their *sons'* or *daughters'* business in the far away United States a waste. Instead, they consider it a useful opportunity to invest in family businesses abroad. However, they have a problem making such contributions when they notice that foreign spouses of such prospective business owners think of such businesses as belonging exclusively to their immediate nuclear families. For fear of this happening, Nigerian parents do not traditionally encourage their sons and daughters to marry outside their ethnic groups.

As part of their ethnic association's obligation, Nigerian immigrants make monthly contributions to a common fund that they can use in handling emergencies, such as the bereavement of a member or his relative, the cost of sending home to Nigeria the remains of dead members and their interment, as well as the cost of gifts given to members during happier occasions, such as naming ceremonies of babies, marriage ceremonies of young couples, and send-off and graduation ceremonies of children and spouses of members. In addition to the emergency funds, the ethnic groups usually set up a rotating credit fund (*Esusu* in Igbo) out of which they grant credits to their members

Naming ceremony. Courtesy of the Christ Apostolic Church of America, Inc., Jamaica, New York.

on a regular basis. The credits have been very helpful to members who need them to establish their own small businesses. They are usually granted with very low interest rates, and each member is given the same repayment conditions. In fact, the associations prefer to grant loans to their members with minimal interest rates to saving their funds in the bank, where much of the interest they accrue is severely taxed by the federal and state governments as well as the bank itself.

Nigerian immigrants who are interested in owning a business have a third avenue through which they can raise necessary capital to start their business. Individuals who cannot afford to raise the required capital on their own can team up with others to put together whatever amounts they have into a common fund that they can all use as capital to found one jointly-owned business. Each of such contributing members put in whatever amount they can afford, the richer members contributing more, but the profit they make from the business is equally shared among all without regard to the amount each contributed toward the capital.

The richer ones do not mind contributing more, because it is part of their cosmological belief that people are richly blessed when they helps their poorer "brothers" to get up, as it were:

A person depends on his agnates "to get up"; they provide social security and comfort. They support his just claims against other groups. They provide the ladder needed in social climbing. It is to one's lineage that a person brings his wife after marriage; it is among his lineage members that he rears his children and gives them their stake in life. Title-taking ceremonies, marriage feasts, second-burial rites, and other ceremonies through which a wider social group is activated succeed or fail because of the type of interpersonal relations between a person and his agnates. (Uchendu 1965, 64–65)

Opportunity Structure Theory. Nigerian entrepreneurs, like any other business owners, are very much aware that, in order to succeed, every business

African American food mart with yams, pounded yam flour, palm oil, and other products for sale. Courtesy of the author.

venture needs good business and managerial acumen, successful mobilization of available resources, and prior identification of reliable markets for the goods the business produces. Because the reasons why Nigerian immigrant entrepreneurs sought to open their own small businesses, and how they mobilized their class, ethnic, and family resources to achieve their ambition has been discussed, what follows is a discussion of the markets—opportunity structures for the immigrant entrepreneurship—which have traditionally patronized their businesses. They include the Nigerian ethnic market and Africana (African, African American, and Afro-Caribbean) minority markets, all of which are sustained by the needs of peoples of African descent in the United States.

The first wave of Nigerian immigrants, who were not used to eating general American food, relied on African American ethnic food, especially those found in the deep southern states, such as North Carolina, South Carolina, Texas, Florida, Louisiana, Georgia, Alabama, and Mississippi, whose special foods serve as part of what people refer to as "southern hospitality." In time, Nigerian immigrants started using such local ingredients as red pepper, collard greens, mustard greens, broccoli, spinach, and vegetable oil instead of fluted pumpkin leaves (*ugu*), bitter leaf (*olugbu*), water leaf (*akwukwo mmiri*), ground hot pepper, and palm oil to prepare soup sources for their foofoo, which they prepared with American rice flour, Bisquick, massa triggo, and farina, instead of Nigerian pounded yam, cassava dough, and garri. However, as the Nigerian immigrant population increased beginning from the 1970s, the immigrants saw the need to import the food items from Nigeria in large quantities. Also, the business owners imported other general merchandise and goods that fall outside the food service areas.

Primarily, Nigerian ethnic markets cater to the needs of Nigerian immigrants in the United States. The items in popular demand are various foodstuffs, music in audio- and videotapes, movies, clothing materials, footwear, handbags, and jewelry. Africana customers are particularly interested in buying from those markets cultural artifacts and religious icons and symbols, such as masked spirits, talking drums, iron gongs, cymbals, and clappers, as well as cowries and waist beads. These items are usually displayed in African or Black Studies offices and Africana homes as a way of affirming their Africanness, especially since the 1970s, when African countries like Nigeria and Ghana successfully organized and hosted Festivals of Black and African Arts and Civilization (FESTAC), which brought together peoples of African descent from Africa, the Americas, Europe, and Oceania. The twenty-fifth anniversary of the event, dubbed FESTAC '77, was hosted by Nigeria. The activities of the festival, such as art exhibitions, lectures, cultural dances, movies, visits to historic sites, especially slave dungeons, and exchange of pleasantries among delegates reunited continental Africans with their long-lost "brothers" and "sisters" from all parts of the world. The convivial atmosphere reminded African Americans of the jubilation that greeted the writers of the Harlem Renaissance (1919–40) in the United States. Nigerian immigrant entrepreneurs watched with keen interest the clothes, the jewelry, books, religious and cultural products, as well as general merchandise that the Africana peoples were interested in, and added them to the types of goods their businesses back home in the United States would be supplying to interested customers.

Over the years, Africana scholars and non-black Africanists have found that their demands for Nigerian/African cultural products and services are easily supplied in Nigerian ethnic markets and stores. The particular services the entrepreneurs provide for their clientele are found in such businesses as Nigerian restaurants, grocery stores, book and video stores, gift shops, beauty salons, and in taxicab and janitorial services. And beginning from the late 1980s, Nigerian immigrants have started professional practice and service in their self-owned businesses, such as law firms, counseling centers, medical clinics, ethnic churches, accounting offices, and insurance agencies. Above all, many of the entrepreneurs have taken to international business operations; they buy and sell American-made goods, such as cars, computers, cameras, TV sets, video games, movies, telephones, and furniture to Nigerians. Also, some of them serve as consultants to American and Nigerian oil companies, which includes promoting good business intercourse between Nigerian and American chambers of commerce.

Most of the Nigerian American businesses are located in black neighborhoods where peoples of African descent live. So, although the business owners may be Nigerian immigrants, the markets are part of the African American market. Many Americans cannot easily identify the immigrants from Africa or the Caribbean in a crowd of black Americans. It is only when they speak that one is able to distinguish them through their accents. Furthermore, the minority markets for Nigerian immigrant goods are also patronized by other American minority groups, like Hispanics and Asians, who are attracted to Nigerian food ingredients and fabrics that closely resemble theirs. In large cities, Nigerian American products attract customers as diverse as the people who live in them.

Like many other new American immigrants, some Nigerians have been successful in mobilizing class, ethnic, and family resources to create wealth out of their self-established small-scale businesses. Apart from identifying the markets that patronize their products, the entrepreneurs have used their busi-

5

Adjustment through Associations and the Media

In the preceding chapter, we noted that Nigerian immigrants receive help from their immediate families and ethnic associations when they first arrive here in the United States, which enables them to adjust quickly to their new society and culture. However, as time goes on, they learn to join other voluntary organizations that cater to their educational, economic, professional, political, and spiritual needs—needs their families and ethnic associations alone cannot provide. That is why they would join other networks through associations, the media, political parties, and organized religious groups in churches, mosques, or temples—networks that play the important role of facilitating immigrant adjustment to all areas of the American life.

This chapter discusses the nature and importance of the various organizations that historically have assisted Nigerian immigrants in their individual and collective efforts to become integrated into all American societies and systems.

ASSOCIATIONS

Because a good number of Nigerian immigrants come to the United States as college or university students, their adjustment and adaptation process begins with their American host families, with whom they make their first contact in the United States and receive their first lessons on the American way of life, before making personal contacts with their academic institutions. On their part, the colleges and universities have to conduct orientation programs for the newcomers through which they are given vital information on all aspects of campus life, and on various voluntary organizations operating within and outside of their campuses. Representatives of the organizations are invited to address the student immigrants on the services that each of them renders to the students and how anyone interested in them can become a member. Initially, the student immigrants show more interest in educational associations, including professional and business organizations, alumni associations, and political organizations, as well as sociocultural and religious groups, which cater to their after-college interests and needs.

Both on-campus and off-campus associations complement the roles that each type plays in the adjustment and adaptation efforts that both student and nonstudent immigrants make to become well-adjusted and integrated members of their society. At any rate, one finds that the roles the associations play in the lives of both kinds of immigrants occur in three phases: the initial phase, when the immigrants first arrive and are helped by members of their immediate families, ethnic associations, and/or American host families (if they are student immigrants); the middle phase, when the newcomers begin their college or university education in the United States until graduation, or until the nonstudent immigrants have successfully found initial jobs to do; and the final phase, when the college and university graduates may have entered the job markets and are struggling to become professionals or successful businesspeople. During this final phase, also, the two kinds of Nigerian immigrants have to make the crucial decision of settling permanently in the United States—a decision that makes it easy for them to adjust and adapt to a society and culture that has been shaped and maintained by older immigrants and native-born Americans.

Educational Associations

Each of the organizations that come under the educational category is multilayered in function and composition. They range from department or program associations, through Greek-lettered organizations and ethnocultural organizations, to the overall student unions of their institutions. All of these associations make good efforts to cater to a variety of adjustment and adaptation needs of student immigrants, which will enable them become in the end a part of the well-trained labor force that every American institution of higher learning contributes yearly to the workforce needs of American businesses in particular, and those of the world communities in general. Certainly, it is imperative that Nigerian immigrants, who come from a third-world country, embrace the vital roles that educational associations play in teaching them how to acquire American libertarian education (offered through science and technology), develop a new work ethic, and understand the concept of the American dream and ways of realizing it.

Department/Program Associations

Every academic department or program in American colleges and universities is obligated to give their students the best academic training and other necessary aids, which enable them to work with relatively few impediments toward earning degrees and diplomas in their chosen fields of study. The faculty members and their supportive staff are there to ensure that that happens, through the instructions they give in the classrooms and labs. But they also encourage their students to form organizations run by the students themselves, who are assisted by graduate and undergraduate faculty advisors. The English department, for example, has two such organizations—the English Association (for undergraduates), and the Association of Graduate Students of English. Each of the two associations works hard to ensure that new students are given directions on how best to pursue their English and literary studies. Also, they are introduced to research skills and to the best Web sites and search engines that can help them find information on electronic and print materials they need whenever they do their assignments. Besides, the executive boards of the organizations, under the aegis of assigned faculty members, regularly organize seminars, conferences, and colloquia in which issues and crosscurrents of literary and language studies are critically examined and discussed. Additionally, graduate students are encouraged to collaborate with their graduate faculty members in writing and presenting papers and articles for presentation in the graduate student caucus of the Modern Language Association, during seminar and conference sessions. As the graduate students attend such academic meetings, they are given the opportunity to observe professors engage in mutual, sometimes explosive, exchange of ideas. And those students who attend the conference regularly and participate actively in the debates do acquire the necessary professional exposure that may prove useful when they start looking for permanent jobs as junior college professors or instructors, after graduation. Their presented and/or published papers and articles and the confidence they may have developed while presenting materials before conference panels go a long way in enabling them to adjust more easily their status as graduate students to instructors and junior professors.

It should be noted, however, that what happens in the English department is applicable to other academic programs and departments of every American university.

Also, through those organizations, students are taught how to prepare curricula vitae (CV) and dossiers according to standard formats of their individual disciplines. Again, under the aegis of designated faculty advisors, the department organizations conduct mock interviews for their junior and senior students, and they are given up-to-date information on job openings in their various disciplines. Most important, each department offers apprenticeship job opportunities to their brightest candidates (when they apply for admission) and to the students who are already enrolled in the program. The apprenticeship jobs include teaching associates or teaching assistants for master's degree candidates and assistant instructors for doctoral degree candidates. Besides, the departments and student organizations have journals, magazines, and newsletters in which their students can publish their articles and papers, which they may cite as relevant and valid experience in their CVs and job applications.

In all cases, student organizations are usually involved in the governance of their individual departments and programs. Some members, especially graduate students, are elected by their peers to sit in faculty committee meetings, such as the new personnel committee and curriculum development committees, without voting rights. But they could form pressure groups from among the student body to lobby the department and program administrators, or even the university administrators, to recruit enough renowned professors to teach courses in their programs. Sometimes, they lobby the department curriculum development committees to create new courses or new areas of specialization, which could complement existing ones in the department. For instance, at Southern Connecticut State University, student bodies have recently been lobbying their department and university administrators to create Human Diversity and Ethnic Studies programs to accommodate the diverse and demographic changes in their student population. In addition, students in other American universities frequently insist that the latest high-tech equipment and teaching aids be provided in their various departments. Usually, the administrators would grant such requests if the overall institutional budget can accommodate them.

These functions and roles played by student associations of academic departments and programs are unfamiliar to Nigerian student immigrants. In fact, some of them are amazed by the apparent equal rights that American faculty and students exercise both in the governance and classroom of their institutions, for in their native Nigeria, students do not have much say in the governance and curricular matters of their institutions. In fact, Nigerian students are reportedly victimized regularly when they criticize professors and administrators, even when their opinions are genuinely offered for the improvement of the students' life and education on campus. Mustering up courage to adjust and adapt to the American "strange" ways becomes a first step that the Nigerian student immigrants must take toward acquiring the libertarian education, which American academic institutions offer to all their students, regardless of their race, gender, or country of origin.

Greek-Lettered Organizations

The educational associations that facilitate Nigerian immigrants' adjustment and adaptation process in this country include graduate and undergraduate organizations that go by Greek letters. They are subdivided into two categories: the scholars' honor societies, and the social fraternities and sororities. Over the years, numerous Nigerian American college graduates have been elected into the Phi Beta Kappa society because of their high academic achievements. The social societies, the fraternities and sororities, are important not only to Nigerian immigrant college students but also to other immigrant students who have no relatives in the United States.

Ethnocultural Student Organizations

When new foreign students arrive on campus, they tend to join any group of people who look like them as they go through the process of adjusting to their new environment. For Nigerian immigrants, those who look like them are African Americans and students from other black African countries and the Caribbean. However, because they are immigrants who have decided to settle permanently in the United States, the necessity to adjust quickly makes them identify initially with African Americans, who are familiar with American culture. For that reason, usually the first ethnocultural organization they join is the Black Student Union, or Africana Student Union. The Nigerian immigrants crave membership in those so they can develop a psychological response to an unfamiliar culture and the ability to acquire new learning, social habits, and mores of their new educational institutions and society.

But in their long-term adaptation process, the immigrants begin to discover that although they may look like African Americans, they are a different ethnic group with different cultural nuances. At that point, they begin to yearn for an ethnocultural organization that is closer to the culture they enjoyed back home in Nigeria before coming to the United States. Again at Southern Connecticut State University, students of African descent (from continental Africa, the Americas, Oceania, and Europe) would normally register their membership initially in the Black Student Union. But as they get gradually adjusted to the social environment, they begin to branch out to join African Student Association or West Indian Academic Society, both of which are on the same campus. And later on, some of them (especially graduate students) would join other ethnocultural student organizations of Greater New Haven area universities, which are composed of students from single countries like Nigeria, Ghana, Sierra Leone, and Kenya. However, students who come from smaller countries usually lack enough members to form separate national organizations, so they may elect to join other ethnocultural groups closest to those of their countries and cultures.

The most prestigious of the Pan-African ethnocultural student organizations in the United States is the Harvard African Law Association, an African graduate student organization seeking solidarity and cooperation among peoples of African heritage at Harvard Law School. According to its first elected president, Ndubisi Obiorah (a Nigerian American), "Harvard African Law Association has the goals of promoting knowledge about law and public policy in Africa among the Harvard Law School community; promoting knowledge of countries, peoples, and cultures of Africa among the Harvard Law School community; and providing a forum for social interaction among African students and students from across the world and the Harvard Law School community. The Harvard African Law Association was formally recognized as an approved student organization by the Harvard Law School on November 6, 2001" (Nwangwu 2002). The goals and objectives of this African graduate ethnocultural organization remind anyone familiar with African political history of similar immeasurable values of the networking and solidarity among the sociopolitical ancestors of Africa like Nnamdi Azikiwe of Nigeria and Kwame Nkrumah of Ghana, who pursued similar goals while studying in the United States and later went home to form and implement the liberation movement of Africa known as Pan-Africanism. Also, they both served as postindependence heads of their respective countries.

More and more Nigerian immigrant students are attracted to their national ethnocultural societies because of the expanding population of students from that country. Yet, with all the good opportunities that the United States offers to them in all areas of their lives, Nigerians still miss the indigenous culture in which they grew. But because they cannot enjoy it fully as they would at home, they are happy to enjoy whatever amount of it that they as an immigrant group can offer to one another.

Nigerian immigrants also acquire valuable information, training, and experience by participating in student government. This facilitates the process of their adjustment and adaptation to their new society while they are still in college and university. As they graduate and leave their alma mater, however, they are encouraged to join other associations that serve as a bridge between college and the wider society.

Alumni Associations

The British government that colonized Nigeria inculcated in the colonial peoples the love of formal education, especially college and university education that produced the first crop of indigenous Nigerian civil servants, educators, and administrators, who played key roles in the governance of the country and the management of its public and private institutions after the British left the country. By 1962, Nigeria had built four universities—the University of Nigeria, Nsukka; University of Ife, Ile-Ife; Ahmadu Bello University, Zaria; and the University of Lagos, Lagos—to add to the premier university college, Ibadan, which was built in 1948 by the British as an overseas campus of the University of London in Great Britain.

The alumni of the five universities saw themselves as a special group of intelligentsia, who must work hard in their various positions in government, education, and the private sector. Also, they became the first middle class of Nigerian workers. The alumni associations they formed were fondly referred to as the "old boys' club" because there were very few female graduates among them. They maintained networks that not only supported their alma maters, but also made sure that their future graduates and children were given decent jobs and positions in the civil service and in higher educational institutions. Also, the alumni carried their interests and roles to the United States when they became immigrants.

The second category of alumni associations is comprised of those that Nigerian students of American universities and colleges subscribe to upon graduation and as they become immigrants. Each alumni association organizes many events every year for their members, such as annual meetings in which the alumni conduct symposia on burning issues of the day, listen to speeches delivered by eminent scholars and prominent people in their fields of expertise, engage in fund-raising activities for worthy causes in their native Nigeria or here in the United States, and enjoy dinners and entertainment that are all arranged by the officers of the association. Through attending those events and meetings, the alumni learn about the achievements and progress of their former classmates and gain useful information on topics, issues, and events that are of critical importance to them. As a network, each association offers members information on job openings for which they could apply, and sometimes some of the members are hired by other members who are chief executive officers of their companies and corporations, while other businesspeople and entrepreneurs may even form partnerships with fellow alumni, who may have become business magnates.

Besides the services the alumni render directly to one another, they make annual monetary and material donations to their alma maters. In fact, some rich members' donations are used to support endowed chairs and lectureships of university departments and programs that attract renowned national and international scholars, as well as generous fellowships and assistantships for their graduate students. In other words, the richer the endowments, the more famous the institution becomes in attracting the best minds, whether as professors or students, that make the institutions great. In return, the universities reward the rich donors with admission and scholarship offers to their sons and daughters, so they can attend the same universities their parents did, thereby maintaining the family tradition, as it were.

The alumni associations' roles go beyond the family circles of the alumni to touch national and international institutions. For instance, at the end of the Nigerian civil war, members of the University of Nigeria, Nsukka, alumni association in the United States contributed money and equipment that were used in rebuilding their war-torn institution in Nigeria. Besides, they helped to secure graduate admissions with teaching assistantships and fellowships for members of their alumni associations in Nigeria. When such alumni arrived, they became members of multiple university alumni associations in the United States. Furthermore, many graduates of American and Nigerian universities developed strong networks that worked hard to establish Nigerian-American university linkages, such as there are between Ohio University in Athens and Ahmadu Bellow University in Zaria, Michigan State University in East Lansing and the University of Nigeria at Nsukka, and the University of Nebraska at Lincoln and the Imo State University at Okigwe. The linked universities have exchange programs for the faculty and students of their respective institutions that have gone a long way in promoting international education and cultural exchange.

Considering their overall services and roles, alumni associations are invaluable organizations for Nigerian immigrants in the United States. They give the immigrants the information they need to find jobs and meet some of the people who create them. The annual meetings they conduct are a great opportunity for social interaction and exposure to some aspects of the new culture that the immigrants have to embrace so as to integrate well into the new society.

Finally, when Nigerian university alumni arrive to join their erstwhile members here in the United States, they give the older Nigerian immigrants news about their native land. In return, the older immigrants give the new ones information on how to survive in their new country. In other words, representatives of Nigerian university alumni associations, who arrive new in the United States, stand to gain a lot from the alumni who came before them and have all the information and the wherewithal that can make the adjustment efforts of the newer immigrants a lot easier. Nigeria benefits in that both categories of Nigerian immigrant alumni have been making a lot of monetary and material contributions to their former universities.

Professional and Business Organizations

The professional and business organizations that Nigerian Americans currently subscribe to are, in the main, those whose memberships are not drawn from Nigerian immigrant population. Unlike other new immigrant groups, Nigerian immigrants did not think of settling permanently here because of their cosmological belief that to emigrate one's country of birth was an act of sabotage to the unity of their three worlds—the physical world of human beings on Earth, the spirit world of the dead-living ancestors below the earth, and the world of the unborn children in the wombs of women. That is to say that if a person settled permanently in the United States, died there, and was buried there, he or she severed relationships with all of the three worlds. So, to make their guilt a little less, many of them put it in their living wills that if they died accidentally in the United States, their remains should be returned to Nigeria and buried there as a way of reuniting them with the dead-living ancestors in the spirit world. Others engaged in return migration once they received a good American education or made enough money to enable them to live comfortably well upon return to Nigeria.

The implication of that kind of belief made it difficult for the Nigerians to decide to settle permanently in the United States until recently, when the realities of Nigerian socioeconomic conditions, as well as the grant of dual citizenship to the immigrants by the governments of the United States and Nigeria, encouraged many new immigrants (including those who lived here before but engaged in return migration) to settle permanently.

In essence, their vacillation in deciding to settle permanently in the United States or to return to their native country delayed the time of their joining American professional and business organizations that could have taught them sooner how to develop their own ethnic or national professional and business organizations. That is why, unlike other new immigrant groups, who made the decision to settle in the United States early, Nigerian immigrants are just beginning to form their own business and professional organizations.

Because many of the immigrants came as graduate students with teaching assistantships and fellowships, and some came as university professors hired directly from Nigeria to develop and teach courses in Africana programs, they helped to create faculty and educational organizations on campuses where they worked. Besides belonging to American national organizations, such as the Modern Language Association of America and the American Psychological Association, the immigrants helped in creating intercontinental organizations like African Literature Association (ALA), African Studies Association (ASA), and National Black Studies Association (NBSA), all of which were, and still are, Afrocentric in conception and function. In time, however, African professors and graduate students needed more outlets and so joined with African American and Afro-Caribbean literary practitioners to form an alternative organization, College Language Association (CLA), and to launch its journal, *CLA Journal.* The organization and its journal thus began to provide the much-needed platform on which African, African American, and Afro-Caribbean issues and topics are fully and hotly debated from season to season.

Nigerian Americans also join professional and business organizations to keep current, find legal support, and to socialize. Considering their functions and roles, the professional and business organizations are a very potent channel through which Nigerian immigrants can obtain the assistance they need for adjustment and adaptation in the United States, especially when they come out of college to begin their business and professional careers. The experience they gain from being members in those organizations is of great help to the immigrants as they make effort to adapt to American business and professional life. That experience is also valuable to those who may engage later in return migration to become great educators, professional leaders, and business gurus. In fact, Nigerian business, educational, and political history is full of names of people whose American experience helped them to make contributions that made a huge difference in Nigerian national, business, economic, and professional life, beginning from the days of Dr. Nnamdi Azikiwe.

But in spite of their belated decision to settle permanently in the United States and form their ethnic business and professional organizations, the Nigerians have made impressive strides beginning from the late 1980s. The improvement made in this area of their immigrant lives is due in part to older Nigerians embracing the new technological culture and the younger generation being born in the United States and educated in American educational systems. As college graduates, many of them were very aware of the importance of belonging to the business and professional associations while they were still in school. Besides, many of them were educated in top business and professional schools; and their membership in the business and professional associations of such schools became a matter of course. After graduation, the more they practice in their businesses and professions, the more they encourage their kith and kin to follow in their footsteps.

Currently, Nigerian immigrants can boast a few but very strong business and professional organizations whose memberships are purely Nigerian. They are formed for the empowerment of their people here in the United States and those in their native Nigeria. They carry out sociocultural functions that are primarily geared toward the development of their villages, clans, ethnic societies, and, very rarely, Nigeria as a whole. The more prominent examples of Nigerian American business and professional organizations working for their people in the United States and Nigeria include the Organization of Nigerian Professions (ONP-USA); Nigerian Business Forum, Inc.; Pro-Health International; Nigerian Professional Network; Songhai Charities, Inc.; African Bar Association of America (ABAA); and Action Against Poverty International, Inc. All of them try to use their technical and professional training and experience to help their communities in the United States and Nigeria in the areas of health care delivery, charitable and legal assistance, private business and industrial development, and poverty alleviation.

From what these organizations have accomplished so far, there is hope that Nigerian Americans will continue to render help to people in both countries. However, that can happen only if more and more of them embrace the business, professional, and technological education and training that the United States offers. Judging from the strides many of them have already made in that direction (as can be seen in the appendix), Nigerian immigrants will soon produce many more business and professional organizations that can render steady services to people in the United States and Nigeria on a regular basis.

Cultural Groups

Before they came to the United States as immigrants, Nigerians enjoyed a variety of celebrations in their native land that produced what their political leaders dubbed "unity in diversity." The celebrations included annual festivals of arts and culture in which dancing troupes from the thirty-six states, and the federal capital in Abuja displayed cultural dances, art exhibitions, literary performances, and lectures to the enjoyment and wonderment of fellow Nigerians and visiting tourists. The 2002 celebrations of the annual festival, for instance, were so colorful and diversified that the Nigerian Tourism Development Corporation devoted a whole booklet to their coverage with a befitting title, *Nigeria: Beauty in Diversity.* Usually, the artists and performers are at their best when they perform in their indigenous languages: lead singers of each ethnic troupe recite the creation story and other major historic events of their people, which constitute their oral history; young men and women engage in phallic dances in which they dramatize male and female rites of passage; talking drums and flutists send esoteric messages to male war dancers who dramatize their prowess and war victories of yesteryears; professional actors and actresses reenact folk rituals and ceremonies in their indigenous languages, which constitute their folk drama; and high school and college students perform plays and recite lyrical poems written in English by contemporary Nigerian playwrights and poets. Nigeria dances as one nation during the festivals, and the convivial atmosphere, more than at any other event in Nigeria, engenders publicly the spirit of unity and nationalism in the people, if only momentarily.

Yet behind the public displays of unity lurk strong ethnic attachments and sentiments that do not augur well for the actualization and maintenance of true nationalism in Nigerian ethnic peoples. Such is the kind of sociocultural legacy that influences the immigrants as they begin to form new national and ethnic sociocultural groups in the United States.

Nigerian immigrant sociocultural organizations can be discussed in three overlapping segments: national, state, and ethnic; and their functions and stated missions can be broadly divided also into three dovetailed categories: entertainment, welfare, and sociopolitical.

Entertainment Organizations

To maintain cultural links with folks in their native land, Nigerian immigrants have been inviting musicians, dancing troupes, and other performing artists from Nigeria to come and perform. Such events usually take place in big cities during the summer months. Over the years, however, many universities, such as Yale, UCLA, Northwestern, Ohio State, Michigan State, and Clark Atlanta, which have strong Africana Studies programs, have been promoting the shows because of their sociocultural, historical, educational, and entertainment values. In addition, the Nigerian immigrants have been collaborating with black civic and political leaders and mayors of cities with large black populations to make the Nigerian cultural shows prominent features of the yearly Black History Month and Kwanza celebrations.

The organizers of the cultural and entertainment shows are usually members of national organizations. The following list gives some ideas of the aims and objectives of some of the immigrants' entertainment groups:

• **Black Sugar Band,** based in Brooklyn, New York, seeks to make Nigerian people happy through music "anytime, any day." http://www.motherlandnigeria.com/organizations.hmtl.

- **Miss Nigeria USA Pageant, Inc.,** out of Atlanta, promotes "Nigeria's rich culture, art and business through the most beautiful and intelligent Nigerian ladies in America." http://www.motherlandnigeria.com/organizations.hmtl.
- **Odenigbo Cultural Group.** This Columbus, Ohio, dance troupe was founded by a renowned professor of African Art History at the Ohio State University, Emmanuel Odita, to promote and perform in the United States famous Igbo cultural dances that have won first place prizes in Nigerian Festival of Arts and Culture competitions. Although most of the dances are Igbo in origin, the dancers and players are Nigerian and African. The group tours the United States, entertaining at major sociocultural events, and has entertained the president of Nigeria, Chief Olusegun Obasanjo, when he came to receive an award at Ohio State.
- **Afro-Gbedu Ensemble** promotes West African music and dance.

Besides the cultural entertainment groups, world-renowned Nigerian immigrants are makers and promoters of their native music, songs, and dance. Among them is Sade, who received a Grammy for Best Pop Vocal Album, *Lovers Rock,* at the forty-fourth annual Grammy awards celebration in 2001. And there are other musicians who are invited so often from Nigeria to perform in the United States that their bands and music are well-known to the American audiences. They include Juju artists such as King Sunny Ade and the African Beats, Ebenezer Obey, and I. K. Dairo and His Blues Spots; Fuji artists like Barrister (Dr.) Sikiru Ayinde; and other artists such as Sonny Okosuns and Sir Stephen Osita Osadebay. But the most revered of the guest artists was Fela Kuti the Afro-Beat King, whose music and songs have inspired since the 1960s black revolutionary artists and political activists in the "three continents" (Africa, North America, the Caribbean) to work for total emancipation of the black man's mental, economic, and political colonization by Western powers.

Welfare Organizations

Virtually all the Nigerian immigrant sociocultural organizations work for educational and socioeconomic developments of their people at the national, state, and local (ethnic) levels. However, their services at all three levels are not mutually exclusive. Instead, the way the services are rendered causes some individual immigrants to belong to multiple service groups. A look at some examples of their missions gives one an insight into the work they have been doing to make Nigerian communities in both countries comfortable to live in or belong to:

- **Association of Nigerians Abroad** is a not-for-profit, nonsectarian organization. But, "whenever necessary, the association advocates democratic ideals, human rights, the rule of law, fairness, justice, and equity in Nigeria and for all Nigerians resident in the United States." http://www.rain.org/~ananet/home.html.

- **Computers to Africa** of Madison, Wisconsin, supports and promotes "computer literacy in Nigeria, by helping with after-school programs, computer schools, and religious organizations in Nigeria." http://www.computerstoafrica.org.

- **Eduwatch** is a nonprofit organization staffed by volunteers based in Gaithersburg, Maryland. It "provides free and/or low cost educational resources to depressed Nigerian schools and educational institutions." http://www.eduwatch.org.

- **Association of Nigerians in Connecticut** was founded to "foster cooperation" among Nigerians who reside in Connecticut. http://www.motherlandnigeria.com/organizations.hmtl.

State and ethnic associations that provide welfare services similar to those stated are Abia State Association, Inc. of New Jersey; Akwa Ibom State Association (USA), Inc.; Calabar Development Association; Alliance of Yoruba Organizations and Clubs; Eastern Nigeria Youth, Inc.; Edo Cultural and Traditional Association; Egbe Omo Yoruba (National Association of Yoruba Descendants); Esan Association, Washington, D.C.; Igbo Cultural and Support Network (ICSN); Igwe Bu Ike (Igbo Cultural Association), Inc.; Ika Community Association; Kwara State Association–USA, Inc.; Kwara State Association of North America, Inc.; the Lagosian; Ndi Igbo in Arkansas; Nwannedinamba; Ogbakor Ikwerre USA, Inc.; Onitsha Abo National Improvement Union; Umunne Progressive Union, Inc.; Umunne Cultural Association of Minnesota; Urhobo Progress Union, North America (UPUNA); Urhobo Congress (USA); and Yoruba Alliance.

Sociopolitical Organizations

The sociopolitical organizations are initially set up by Nigerian Americans to foster ethnic unity and the sociocultural, economic, and educational development of their members and their societies. In time, however, some of the sociocultural groups would develop into powerful political organizations, which work for particular politicians, geopolitical regions, and the overall political ascendancy of their particular ethnic peoples in Nigeria. For that reason, membership in each of them could be regional, national, and international, as the case may be. The North American branches of the ethnic sociopolitical organizations tend to be more sophisticated in their operations as a result of what some of them learned from American geopolitical practice. Besides, the money they donate to their national headquarters in Nigeria is usually larger than those given by other overseas branches from Europe, Asia, and Africa, because of the riches of Nigerian Americans and the strength of the U.S. dollar over other world currencies.

Furthermore, the sociopolitical powers of the organizations tend to reflect the numerical, political, financial, and administrative strengths of the ethnic peoples of Nigeria. The most notable of the organizations are Egbe Omo Yoruba (National Association of Yoruba Descendants), World Igbo Congress (WIC), and Zumunta Association–USA. Each of them is an extension of a well-known organization in Nigeria.

World Congress of Afenifere, for instance, is an offshoot of the powerful Pan-Yoruba Egbe Omo Yoruba. The United States branch of the World Congress of Afenifere is located in New York City The organization is committed to serve the socioeconomic and sociocultural needs of the Yoruba people in Nigeria and elsewhere in the world. It is a service that includes contributing positively to the self-improvement, the educational and technological advancement, and the overall welfare of the people.

World Congress of Afenifere is one of the most politically powerful Nigerian ethnic organizations in the United States. The Yoruba demonstrated their ethnic unity and political prowess when, in 1993, they mobilized (Alliance of Yoruba Organizations and Clubs) to fight the cancellation of the Nigerian presidential election that a Yoruba candidate, Bashorun M. K. O. Abiola, reportedly won. Through their daily demonstrations in Washington, D.C., and New York, the Yoruba sociopolitical organization so roused the political consciousness of the United Nations and the United States toward Nigerian geopolitics that both powers got involved in condemning and working against the cycle of military administrations in that country, which were headed by Hausa/Fulani warlords. In the end, another Yoruba man, Chief Olusegun Obasanjo, was democratically elected the postmilitary era president of Nigeria in May 1999 with the help of the United States government. The vigorous campaigns mounted by Egbe Omo Yoruba, the money they contributed, the administrative and strategic prowess they exhibited, and the ethnic unity they forged all combined to actualize the Yoruba collective determination to have one of their own become (for the first time in Nigerian history) president of postcolonial Nigeria—a post that the other two major ethnic groups, the Igbo and the Hausa/Fulani, had occupied in the past.

Like Egbe Omo Yoruba, World Igbo Congress is an offshoot of the Pan-Igbo sociopolitical organization, Ohanaeze Ndigbo. Founded in Houston, Texas, in 1999, WIC's major goal is to promote solidarity and togetherness of Igbo people in diaspora, a goal that derives from their time-tested apothegm, *Igwe Bu Ike* ("Unity Is Strength"). While pursuing that goal, the organization has recorded many sociocultural achievements, such as being able to unify and direct other national, state, and local organizations so that the contributions they make individually and collectively toward the general welfare and development of their societies and people can yield positive and effective results; helping to establish Igbo centers in North America where Igbo children and others are taught Igbo language, culture, and civilization; making financial, equipment, and other material donations that enhance the quality of life and education in Igboland; and establishing Igbo Credit Union in the United States, whose facilities and resources promote and support the economic empowerment of their people.

Serving as a sociopolitical organization, World Igbo Congress has made good strides in working with, and giving moral and financial support to, the parent organization at home, Ohanaeze Ndigbo: by providing counsel and financial support to Igbo delegation to the Nigerian National Constitution Conference in 1995; by developing a program to rehabilitate Biafran War veterans, and seeking ways of establishing a befitting memorial to the victims of that war, as well as to the victims of ethnic cleansing and pogrom meted against Igbo people by fellow Nigerians before and after the Civil War; and, by their commitment to resolving the conflicts of Igbo political leaders, and promoting their political ambitions regardless of their individual parties, so as to make the Igbo the political beacon they were to other Nigerians before the Nigeria-Biafra War.

Zumunta Association—USA is a sociopolitical organization of Northern Nigerians based in New York. Like its Western Nigerian (World Congress of Afenifere) and Eastern Nigerian (World Igbo Congress) counterparts, Zumunta is an offshoot of a formidable Northern Nigerian sociopolitical group, Arewa Consultative Forum. Zumunta aspires to help develop the Northern Nigeria technologically, socially, and economically, "cater for members, preserve the rich and diverse culture of Nigeria, and improve the image of the country in the global arena" (http://www.zumunta.org).

Zumunta works toward computer literacy by donating computers, printers, books, and gadgets to Northern Nigerian schools. Zumunta also pays for students to go to selected Nigerian universities to study science, medicine, engineering, and vocational education.

NEWSPAPERS AND OTHER MEDIA

Nigerian Americans have learned from other new immigrants to publish in English their own newspapers—in print and on-line—which provide information on their communities in the United States and Nigeria. That way they create the atmosphere of a home away from home. The newspapers are used as a means of refuting the negative news generally created by most American mass media about Nigerians in both countries. Also, the newspapers serve as a ready and cheap means through which Nigerian immigrant entrepreneurs advertise their goods and products to their target customers. That is why some of the newspapers, especially the free ones, are displayed in Nigerian, African, African American, and Caribbean grocery stores, supermarkets, and bookstores, where readers can purchase them as they shop for other Nigerian merchandise. However, except for one or two of them, the newspapers have not been sold on general American newsstands until recently, so their circulation is often local and limited.

History of Nigerian Newspapers in the United States

Nigerian American newspapers have a short history in the United States. From the 1970s through the late 1980s, Nigerians received information about their former country and its peoples through the newspapers published in that country, which were brought into the United States by visiting immigrants, and by Nigerian diplomats who displayed them in their embassy in Washington, D.C., Consulate General Office in New York, and consular offices in Atlanta, Chicago, and Los Angeles. Nigerians who lived outside those cities could not access the information the newspapers carried until the 1990s, when they began to do so on-line. So the next best thing they did to receive the news from Nigeria was that those who read the news from papers brought in through the two means described previously disseminated it through telephone conversations.

Furthermore, some enterprising immigrants who lived in places where the newspapers were available began developing and publishing newspapers that carried news about Nigeria that they received and synthesized from all the news cast by Voice of Nigeria, Voice of America, the BBC, and CNN, as well as Nigerian dailies such as *Daily Times, Vanguard,* the *Guardian,* and *Post Express.* Two such premier Nigerian American newspaper are *Nigerian Times International* and *African Enquiry,* published in New York, which are no longer in circulation but have made way for *African Sun Times,* which is now sold on U.S. newsstands.

Nigerian immigrants were also interested in news about other African countries, especially those in the West African subregion. So they collaborated with other African immigrant publishers and reporters to publish news about African politics, economy, health care, education, and immigration matters in newspapers that carried important information on those issues, which are of common interest to all African immigrants in the United States. For example, one of such Pan-African newspapers in circulation is *African Abroad,* whose publishers are also Nigerians. Its February 28, 2002, edition carried such topical news items as "900 Nigerians and Ghanaian Arrested...Face Deportation," "Angola: The End of Savimbi," "Sierra Leone: Commissioner Turns Down Top Police Post," "Last Honor for Ige [the assassinated Nigerian attorney-general] in New York," "Nigeria Rules Out Foreign Coach," "Immigration: Who Qualifies for 'Late Amnesty'?" and news tidbits that come under "Africa News Roundup," "Opinion," "Ghana Headlines," "Sierra Leone Update," "Nigeria News Roundup," and "Mediawatch."

Beginning from the mid-1990s, Nigerian entrepreneurs have also been publishing newspapers on-line. The most renowned of such publishers is Chido Nwangwu, who has numerous Web sites and pages, including "*USAfricaonline.com,* the first African-owned, U.S.-based professional newspaper ever published on the Internet which carries excerpts from *USAfrica The Newspaper.* Published since May 11, 1994, on the 2nd and 4th Wednesdays of every month, *USAfricaonline.com* is the highest-circulation newspaper serving the rapidly growing vibrant community and business demographic mix of immigrant Africans, African Americans, and other Americans" (Nwangwu, *USAfricaonline.com*). Nwangwu has other newspapers on-line that cover national and international topics, such as oil business, the economy, immigration, and race relations in the United States, as well as geopolitical and ethnic clashes in Nigeria. The sites are NigeriaCentral.com, BBJonline.com, PetroGasWorks, and the *Black Business Journal* newspaper.

The Politics of Nigerian American Newspapers

The negative image of Nigeria, as published in American mass media, was largely due to the general corruption, hedonism, debauchery, and other social offenses like denial of fundamental human rights, false arrests, and imprisonment, which successive Nigerian military juntas committed against their own citizens from 1970 through 1999. However, when some Nigerian Americans attempted to respond to some of the issues raised in major American national newspapers, their written opinions were never published; many felt that this was because mainstream American publishers did not give serious consideration to such opinions or that they did not have regard for the Nigerian writers, who were not syndicated columnists. Without any challenges from those mostly affected by the news, the American media continued to publish news that tarnished the image of Nigeria, as it also vilified directly and indirectly Nigerians in diaspora, including the Nigerian Americans.

Nigerian government agencies created damage control units in their diplomatic offices in the United States and in other countries. The News Agency of Nigeria (NAN) opened offices in New York and Washington, D.C., to give a positive spin on the image of Nigeria. The more that happened with the urging and approval of such ruthless military rulers like Abacha, Babangida, and Buhari (who sponsored the spins with Nigerian oil money), the more the world was prevented from knowing the truth about the atrocities committed against the people. And the few courageous journalists like Dele Giwa, who told the gory stories of Nigeria in their newspapers and magazines as they saw them, were either assassinated or sent to jail where nobody could see or talk to them. In fact, many of them perished in jail without any of their family members or relatives being allowed to find out what killed their loved ones. And so the Nigerian papers in the United States, which initially appeared apolitical, began to take a more activist stance in their news reports.

The political activism of some of the newspapers came to a head in 1993 when they served as platforms on which Nigerian Americans stood to condemn General Abacha's cancellation of the results of the election of a civilian candidate, Bashorun M. K. O. Abiola, as the next civilian president of the Federal Republic of Nigeria. The papers so mobilized Nigerians at home and abroad that there were spontaneous demonstrations in the major cities of the United States, Nigeria, Canada, and in many European countries. Although General Abacha used the military to crush the demonstrations in which many people lost their lives (an ugly event memorialized yearly in Nigeria as "June 12th" since 1994), the success the people recorded invigorated them to do more in bringing about a democratic government in Nigeria. In the end, members of the Black Caucus, Congress itself, and the then president of the United States, Bill Clinton, heard Nigeria's cry and gave Nigerians the moral and material support that enabled them to conduct successful local elections in 1998, and state and federal elections in 1999, which ushered in a civilian regime beginning with the Obasanjo administration in May 1999.

Other Media

As a result of the education they have acquired during this age of information technology, Nigerian Americans are enabled at last to use other media available to them as means of communication and entertainment. They include the Internet, television, movies, as well as video- and audiotapes, which are faster, more convenient, and easier than newspapers to disseminate news and entertainment to Nigerian communities in the United States and Nigeria. Although the immigrants use the Internet and television as useful alternatives to the print media in the United States for getting the news, they depend heavily on movies, videotapes, and audiotapes imported from Nigeria for entertainment.

The Internet. The Internet has made it not only possible but very easy for Nigerian immigrants to communicate with their people and others all over the world through e-mail. Chief among the frequently used Web sites and pages for Nigerian papers by Nigerians in the United States are the following:

- **Abuji Mirror,** a weekly. http://www.ndirect.co.uk/~n.today/mirror.html.
- **The Guardian-Nigeria,** a liberal newspaper. http://www.nigerianews.net/.
- **Post Expressed Wired,** an independent Nigerian paper. http://www.post expresswired.com/.
- **The Nigeria News Network.** http://www.nigerianews.net.
- **Nigeria Today.** http://www.nigeriatoday.com/.
- **Nigeria-Nigeria Exchange-Nigerian Newspapers.** http://www.nigerian galleria.com/news/news.htm.
- **Nigerian Investment Promotion Commission.** http://www.nipc-Nigeria.org/.
- **Nigeriaworld-All About Nigeria.** http://www.nigeriaworld.com/.

All these Web sites and pages have been making it easy for some Nigerians who are dual citizens to get direct information from their second country. Also, through the electronic media, it has been easy for scholars and researchers of African and Nigerian studies in the United States to access information and exchange ideas with their counterparts in Nigeria and elsewhere in the world.

Television. The Nigerian American community does not have their own television programming yet. But their scholars and businesspeople appear on Black Entertainment (BET) stations, CNN, and other cable network stations to discuss issues that affect them as a people in the United States and Nigeria. Also, CNN has been employing reporters of Nigerian descent (e.g., Michael Okwu in the United States, and others in Nigeria) to cover news on Nigeria, Africa, and the United States for broadcast on their television stations. Through the use of satellite, Nigerian television stations have been taking some news and entertainment from CNN and other cable networks in the

United States, as well as those from the BBC in England for regular features in their daily broadcasts. Their audience finds news about international politics, the economy, and business, as well as American soap operas especially interesting to watch.

Movies, Video-, and Audiotapes. Nigerian immigrants watch American-made movies primarily for entertainment and secondarily for instruction. Watching television to relax, they also watch movies made on various aspects of American national life to imbibe the ways of life of their new neighbors. Such instructive movies can facilitate their adaptation and adjustment process. This second type of movies are purchased and viewed over and over again by the immigrants, especially college students majoring in English, theater, art, social work, political science, and communications, who may need the movies in doing their course assignments.

Lately, Nigerian film directors and home moviemakers have been producing movies that look more and more like American soap operas and sitcoms, which they export to the United States and Europe. Virtually all of them are for entertainment, even though they are didactic in tone. But the videos that Nigerians buy most frequently are those depicting cultural dances, folk stories and tales, and rituals and ceremonies that constitute their traditional folk drama. As most of them are recorded during Nigerian festivals of art, when Nigeria as a nation dances, playing them during similar social occasions in the United States gives Nigerians some sense of fellow-feeling with people in Nigeria. Also, it provides a type of group therapy and psychic escape to those who terribly miss their native land. Nevertheless, the celebrative events from Nigeria are also recorded in audiotapes and exported to the United States.

Whether one buys them for entertainment and/or instruction, the Nigerian movies, video- and audiotapes have been used by Nigerian American parents as invaluable aids for instructing their children on their Nigerian roots. Some of the children are so enamored with the contents of the movies and tapes that they insist on being taken to Nigeria for vacations so they can celebrate the events live with family and relations. And after their initial visits, many of them have asked for permission from their parents and school authorities to go live with their Nigerian grandparents and cousins for a year or two because of their appreciation and enjoyment of the life, customs, and people of Nigeria.

To sum up, the various associations, newspapers, and other forms of media discussed can help Nigerian immigrants to adjust to American ways. Various associations and newspapers and the electronic media have helped Nigerian Americans to acquire information on their new country and the world at large, enabling them to lead a more enlightened and productive, and therefore fuller, life in the United States. Although adjustment and adaptation to this country are ongoing processes, the extent to which an immigrant or a group of immigrants has adjusted their lives in the new social order can be measured by the positive contributions they make to society. So, judged by that criterion, Nigerian immigrants are adjusting well to all aspects of American national life.

6

Intergroup Relations

The processes of adjustment and adaptation of Nigerian immigrants to their new environment we have so far discussed involve maintaining good, healthy relations with other Americans of different sociocultural backgrounds. Through continuous new learning, trial and error, and more learning, Nigerians have been finding ways of carrying out their life activities with increasing ease, confidence, and proficiency to the extent that they currently occupy key positions in almost all government and private-sector institutions. For those of them who have made the awesome decision to live permanently here in the United States, however, the necessity for full adaptation to the American way of life is often comprehensive and all-consuming. For that reason, Nigerians are of necessity bound to develop intergroup relations in their everyday living; sometimes this turns out well, but other times cultural conflicts occur.

The cultural conflicts Nigerian immigrants experience with their new neighbors (just like other new Americans do) are inherent in immigration itself as a social institution. That is why, like most other social institutions, immigration has its economic, political, biological, and historical aspects. The general problems of cultural conflicts and adjustments so characteristic of immigration fall into the field of social studies.

Specifically, however, this chapter discusses Nigerian Americans' relations with white Americans, with African Americans, and with other African immigrants, such as Ghanaians, South Africans, Cameroonians, and Liberians in the United States. But the discussion is predicated upon the assertion that "human nature is everywhere the same and everywhere different. Call this a paradox, if you will. Everywhere we find identical units of behavior regarded as essentially human—religions, manners, language, morals, etc.—hence human nature is everywhere the same so far as the number of units is concerned. However, since these units of behavior tend to vary in content in various situations because they have developed in different cultural complexes, human nature differs everywhere" (Brown 1969, 1). The exploration of why human nature is simultaneously the same and different everywhere should help people to understand why Nigerian intergroup relations with any of the named groups of Americans fluctuate like tidal waves of the sea.

RELATIONS WITH WHITE (EUROPEAN) AMERICANS

The discussion of Nigerian immigrants' relations with white Americans begins with a historical overview of majority Americans' image of minority Americans of African descent. That image, which is rooted in history, created black-white relations that began on unequal footing. Such historic world events as slavery, the scramble for Africa, and colonialism combined to make it all too easy for whites in Europe and the Americas to play the role of masters over Africans in diaspora, whom they colonized, enslaved, and dehumanized for many centuries. Whether as colonized peoples in continental Africa or slaves in the Americas, blacks were expected to accept a lower racial rank in those societies. Many whites who have such history-based expectations of all blacks (including those who are now living in their independent countries), have argued that their ancestors were the first immigrants to come to the United States. Through the battles they fought with Native Americans, they acquired virtually all parts of the country now called the United States of America, before they brought in Africans to work for them as slaves. Furthermore, only the slaves in the Confederate states still fighting in the Civil War were freed in 1863, when President Abraham Lincoln signed the Emancipation Proclamation. All slaves in the United States were not freed until the Thirteenth Amendment to the Constitution was ratified on December 6, 1865. And toward the end of the nineteenth century, European whites scrambled for and partitioned Africa into colonies that they governed up to the late 1960s. That is why whites (whether Americans of European descent or colonists in Africa of European descent) have claimed superior social, economic, political, racial, and religious authority over all Americans of African descent.

At first, the minority status accorded to all nonwhites, especially blacks, did not seem to bother Nigerians, who felt they could endure the low status for a while and then return to their native Nigeria, where it appears "all men are created equal" because, in that society, everybody is black. However, as more and more of them decided to settle permanently in the United States, they inherited the minority status of the native-born blacks: the African Americans. Besides, there was no serious need for distinguishing between black people from various parts of the world and American blacks until the 1980s, when the number of African immigrants became substantial. Racial profiling and indiscriminate shooting by white police officers affected all blacks in the United States; but it was (and still is) worse on African blacks, who could not exercise their legal rights like American blacks in the form of protests against being shot by law enforcement officers for minor "provocations," against false arrests and imprisonment, and against being deprived of their individual or group liberties and social justice.

Some of the social and legal problems of Nigerian immigrants in the United States emanate from the misinformation and disinformation on Africa and its peoples that writers of history and literature sold to innocent white Americans (and Europeans), which were accepted as truth. For example, one early European colonial writer, Joseph Conrad, popularized the notion that Africa was "the heart of darkness" in his work, *Heart of Darkness* (1902). In that novella, African characters are delineated as savages, heathens, and caricatures of people; but white characters are depicted as imperial, adventurous, and civilizing people—characteristics that unsophisticated readers are most likely to get out of the narrative without apprehending the central themes of the book, which are the hypocrisy and absurdity of the white man's adventures in precolonial and colonial Africa.

The sordid image of Africa, which was first established by early Portuguese travelers and popularized later by Conrad, encouraged whites in the United States and Europe to go to the so-called benighted continent to colonize and buy its peoples as slaves and to turn them into chattel. And when their heinous activities were challenged, even the Christian slave traders among them offered the subterfuge that they engaged in the trade as a means of saving the benighted souls of Africans from burning in hell fire, without any reference whatsoever to their own greedy commercial interests. But their subterfuge could not withstand the test of time. In fact, from the commentary of a white editor of the novella, Paul O'Prey, the greedy intent of the white man's exploration of the African continent is unmistakable:

> However, by the time Conrad reached the Congo, it had become the virtual private property of Leopold and the good work accomplished in

the names of Christianity and Progress had been all but forgotten in the stampede of fortune hunters. This had resulted in what were, perhaps, the most appallingly greedy, cruel and hypocritical acts of colonial exploitation of the nineteenth century and what Conrad, in his essay, "Geography and Some Explorers," called "the vilest scramble for the loot that ever disfigured the history of human conscience and geographical exploration." (from Conrad 1983, 12)

Furthermore, the *Tarzan* saga of early motion pictures, which are still being rerun in both their original and cartoon versions, continue to fossilize that image of Africa as a dark continent in the minds of some Americans who have never visited Africa or had any close contact with educated Africans (including Nigerian Americans) in the United States.

During the 1960s and 1970s, Nigerian immigrants and white Americans got along because neither considered the other a threat. The Nigerians were busy going to school, which enabled them to potentially find good jobs in the United States, if they decided to settle permanently, or empowered them to occupy government positions in Nigeria, if they returned home. On the other hand, the white Americans did not seem to care much about what the Nigerians did, as long as their jobs and security were not threatened, and their superior positions and authority in society were not in any way impugned. Also, in the academic institutions, Nigerian graduate students and professors provided the much-needed diversity in student populations and curricular offerings, especially in the arts and social sciences. Many of the students in those two decades came with Nigerian federal and state scholarships, in addition to those who came to study on private sponsorships of their rich parents and other relatives. American institutions were happy to welcome Nigerians to their campuses for the cultural diversity they provided, for the money the students paid for their education, and for the curricular contributions of Nigerian professors and scholars. Furthermore, the students came with F-1 visas, and the visiting professors with J-1 visas. Neither of the two kinds of visa guaranteed their holders a long stay in the country. And those who came with green cards were very, very few then. For all those reasons, Nigerians were not a financial burden to the U.S. government, nor could they as noncitizens seek social amenities, even if they were too poor to live in the United States. Besides, they could not mount any serious legal challenges against those who treated them wrongly for fear of deportation, lest they be perceived wrongly or rightly as troublemakers. That fear was especially real to those who needed to apply for a change of their visa status, from F-1 to green card, and for citizenship.

In addition, the first generation of Nigerian immigrants in the United States were older in age, better educated, and more disciplined than the younger generation. For those reasons, they were less likely to flout immigration laws or commit crimes that could send them to jail or cause their deportation back to Nigeria. Any violations of the American laws or university rules and regulations could cause them to fail in achieving their aims. So they constantly reminded each member of their immigrant group to be law-abiding all the time they were in this country.

The discipline they acquired in Nigeria before coming to the United States helped them to become model students, in that they were always respectful of the constituted authorities of the institutions they were attending, and they also devoted most of their time and effort on school work. Furthermore, the Nigerian immigrants' educational success emanates from the overall hard life and competitive nature of the Nigerian society and academic institutions, which had toughened and prepared them for competing with American and other foreign students.

Upon graduation from university, many Nigerian students received good reference letters from their white professors, which enabled them to land good jobs. The very disciplined life they led in the universities continued to enable them to serve as good and dedicated employees wherever they worked. In addition, white employers helped their Nigerian workers to obtain permanent visas that enabled them to bring their family members who were still living in Nigeria over to the United States. Churches and other social institutions also helped in that effort.

Things started to fall apart, however, for both groups when many of the Nigerian immigrants received higher university degrees, became American citizens, and sought the same jobs and higher positions that white Americans had held exclusively for decades without any serious challenges and competition from any of the minority groups of Americans. Furthermore, Nigerian immigrants became very conscious of exercising their rights as citizens and used available Nigerian American lawyers to assist them as they sought legal remedies and justice in court, whereas hitherto there had been some socioeconomic and occupational deprivations. Even those who were not yet citizens but worked with green cards learned from their family lawyers that it was illegal for their employers to pay them salaries that were lower than those paid to their white counterparts who held comparable jobs. But as jobs became more scarce, competition for the few available openings became more acute. Some of the Nigerians who still had their jobs were not promoted when they deserved to be, while others were laid off before their white colleagues. With heightened frustration and disillusionment, some of them filed lawsuits against their white employers for racial discrimination. In the end, the erstwhile good relations between Nigerian and white Americans became shaky to the point that some white benefactors could no longer sponsor as many applications for travel visas of Nigerian immigrants' families as they did when relations were more cordial. Also, it was at this point that some Nigerian immigrants, who could not be reunited with their families in the United States (due to lack of visa for such family members), returned to Nigeria.

Another factor that caused some degeneration in Nigerian immigrants' relations with whites is the clash between some Nigerian and white American professors and scholars over the issue of who is a better interpreter of African literary writings and sociocultural studies. This situation came to a head when some Nigerian (and other African) scholars began to seriously question the type of critical reviews and evaluations from some white critics of literary and sociocultural studies by Nigerian writers. Some Nigerian critics believed that their insiders' knowledge of the sociocultural issues that Nigerian writers wrote about, as well as their professional training in the field, gave them some advantage over the white critics, whom they considered outsiders. A classic example of the debate is one that was sparked off by Ernest N. Emenyonu's 1971 essay titled, "African Literature: What Does It Take to Be Its Critic?" In it, Emenyonu took Bernth Lindfors (a white critic of African literary works) to task for expressing what Emenyonu considered a low opinion of Cyprian Ekwensi's art. Responding to that charge, Lindfors defended his opinion by offering detailed textual evidence of the low quality of Ekwensi's art. This he did in the article he titled, "The Blind Men and the Elephant," which metaphorically referred to how Emenyonu had been too blinded by his close relationship with Ekwensi to see the artistic flaws in the writer's works (Lindfors 1999, 1–16).

In this kind of debate, the audience is drawn to one side or the other. However, Africa's foremost novelist, Chinua Achebe, contended that the claim of intellectual authority by Nigerian and American scholars on African literary (and sociocultural) studies is earned by the serious work, diligence, commitment, and responsibility of a scholar in his or her chosen field of studies. Race, ethnicity, skin color, or any other types of claim not based solely on scholarship is extraneous and, therefore, irrelevant (Ogbaa 1981).

In the government sphere, Nigerian immigrants in the United States have been severely affected over the years by foreign policies made by various U.S. administrations, and by the foreign bills enacted by Congress that are unfavorable to Nigeria and other black African nations. Beginning from the 1960s, white people in Europe and the United States started reacting negatively to the good fight that most African nation-states were fighting to gain political independence from their erstwhile European colonial masters. And in the 1970s and 1980s, when the Soviet Union attempted to spread Communism all over the African continent, the United States decided to arm the leaders of those who opposed their African government that accepted to experiment with Communism as a viable alternative system to the Western colonial rule that they had been subjected to as colonized peoples. Through the indigenous collaborators, the United States and the Soviets found a foothold to recolonize Africa mentally, economically, and socially—a system that social scientists call Neocolonialism. In the end, the United States and its allies began covert operations against the Soviet Union for sociopolitical and economic control of African countries, which had just gained their independence from Europe.

Ostensibly, the Soviets had gone to sub-Saharan Africa to spread Communism, and Americans went there to contain what they regarded as "evil empire" and to impose their brand of democracy. In the process, each of the two superpowers created warlords that favored their ideology and armed them to the teeth so that whoever destroyed a rival warlord in a given country imposed the particular sponsoring superpower's ideology. In time, the Soviets left Africa rapidly; without a rival power to do battle with, the Americans also left. But both superpowers left behind them heavy weapons and munitions, as well as diametrically opposed political ideologies, for their dictator stooges, who used them to fight and destroy their own citizens.

Thus, Africa was militarized and once again depopulated in the twentieth century by whites, just as the Europeans (whites) did during the eras of the partition of Africa and the slave trade. Those heavy weapons not only killed Africans in Somalia, Eritrea, and Ethiopia, they also killed American soldiers in the 1990s when they went on the mission "Operation Provide Hope" in Somalia. Americans were highly offended when they saw the images of such killings on TV. In response to the situation, many white Americans began attacking African blacks verbally, emotionally, and sometimes physically, without regard to their individual countries of origin.

Despite such indiscriminate attacks, Nigerian immigrants and visitors in this country remained relatively calm and law-abiding. Instead, some have always encouraged the Nigerian diplomatic mission in the United States to sell more oil to the United States so as to offset the shortfall in oil supplies that usually follow the Middle East crises. In response to such gestures by Nigerian immigrants and diplomats, Congress and the White House (especially during the Reagan and Bush I administrations) avoided engaging in any healthy political intercourse with Nigeria, preferring instead to punish it as a country ruled by military dictators and a place where civil rights abuse is rampant. When some members of the Black Caucus in Congress attempted to go on a fact-finding mission to Nigeria, they were vilified for "fraternizing" with dictators. This was the case with Senator Carol Moseley-Braun of Illinois, whose visit to Nigeria with General Sani Abacha in 1998 was used as a campaign issue that contributed in no small measure to her defeat when she ran for a second term in office.

Furthermore, for nearly two decades, Congress and the presidency have banned the Nigerian National Airways carriers from flying in and out of the United States, ostensibly because they regard Nigeria as a totalitarian country even though Nigeria has been ruled by a civilian president since May 1999. In the face of the ban, Nigerian immigrants and visitors are further humiliated when they fly. Those traveling with Nigerian passports are systematically asked to form isolated lines for vigorous, often humiliating searches by law-enforcement officers. This profiling of Nigerian air travelers began before, and has increased after, the September 11, 2001, incidents, despite the fact that no Nigerian immigrant or visitor to the United States has ever been accused of taking part in terrorist acts.

The foreign policies that Congress and the White House have been adopting over the years toward black countries, especially Nigeria, are clearly inimical to Nigerian American–white American relations.

Nigeria and other black African countries are of national security and strategic interest to the United States. Nigeria contributed a large number of soldiers to the United Nations Forces during "Operation Desert Storm" and during the peacekeeping and peacemaking campaigns in Somalia, Bosnia, Sierra Leone, and Liberia. In fact, Nigerian military commanders led the United Nations Forces that successfully ended the civil wars in Sierra Leone, as well as helped it to conduct a successful postwar elections that ushered in a democratic regime in 2002.

Economically, Nigeria supplies 17 percent of the oil that the United States imports. Also, Nigeria supplanted the oil supplies to the United States from the Middle East that were temporarily halted as a result of the 1967 and 1973 Arab-Israeli wars. And in 2002, when the Arabs threatened to use withholding of oil as a weapon against the United States if Saddam Hussein and Iraq were attacked, President Obasanjo of Nigeria was summoned to Washington for talks with President Bush on contingency plans for more oil supplies from that country, should the Arabs carry out their threats. Nigeria is a powerful member of OPEC and has continued to play a mediating role between the United States and the Arab members of the oil cartel.

Nigerian immigrants in the United States and Nigerians at home are grateful to former President Clinton for bringing to focus the sub-Saharan African subregion to American foreign policy debates. He not only toured many African countries in his second term in office but also helped to bring about a democratic government in Nigeria in 1999. Like his predecessors in office, he was critical of the Nigerian military regimes that ruled Nigeria from 1966 to 1999, but he did something positive about it. And with the general assistance of the Black Caucus in Congress, as well as that of General Colin Powell before and after he became secretary of state, Nigeria is now belatedly recognized as a country that is strategically and economically important to the United States.

On the whole, the Nigerian immigrants' relations with white Americans are dynamic, and they are heavily affected by events of past history, namely racism and colonialism.

RELATIONS WITH AFRICAN AMERICANS

Relations between Nigerian Americans and African Americans are more than skin deep. These two groups of Americans are blood relatives who also are connected by their minority status in the United States, with all its sociopolitical and economic ramifications. For example, both groups are victims of racial profiling by the police. Does that then mean that their intergroup relations are good and smooth all the time? Certainly not. This discussion of the relations of the two black relatives in the United States must take into account such factors as black history, social culture, educational attainment, and sociopolitical ambitions, which affect the way each group behaves toward the other in a given time period or circumstance.

The Nigerians who came to the United States during the first two waves of their immigration (1925–80) were warmly welcome by African Americans. Their first meetings were as emotional as the reuniting of long-separated family members. After the initial euphoric encounter, however, African Americans, who are descendants of African slaves, began to express mixed emotions: On the one hand, they were very happy to receive their distant cousins from Africa and anxious to hear stories of the slave trade that had kept both groups apart for so long. On the other hand, some were very unhappy that Africans allowed the whites to buy their ancestors, whom they used as chattel. Their anger soon turned into envy, sorrow, and rage when they realized that some of the arriving Nigerians were better educated than many of them were. In their native country, Nigerians had access to education without the impediments of the Jim Crow law that prevented many African Americans from learning to read and write in the southern states of the country up to the 1920s. But the version of the stories of the slave trade and slave raids that educated Nigerians and other Africans told managed to assuage the rage and sorrow of many African Americans.

What later became the slave trade was originally genuine trade by barter between Africans and enterprising Europeans who were interested in African natural and crafted goods, such as gold, spices, ivory, elephant tusks, cowries, mats, and pottery. In exchange, Africans received from the Europeans manufactured goods, such as alcohol (especially whiskey), clothing, and trinkets. At the end of each day's purchases, European traders asked their African trade partners to order their young men and women to help them carry the goods they purchased to their boats on the seashores. The chiefs and elders obliged, and the young people were given gifts like sleeveless shirts and sugar for their services—gifts that encouraged others to join their peers in carrying more goods to the boats. In time, the conniving white traders established some measure of trust from both the African elders and the youth, only to betray the trust later by turning the young people into captives who later became the first African slaves in the Western world. After waiting for the return of their sons and daughters beyond the time it normally took the children to return, able-bodied men armed themselves with bows and arrows and machetes to go in search of their missing children. Of course, at that time, the white slave traders would have set sail for Europe and the Americas. As the slave traders returned to Africa, they initially avoided the places they had been before for fear of being discovered. But as they got bolder and bolder in the business, they returned to places they had been before. Naturally, the affected African communities attacked the first whites they saw, but in all cases, the whites outmaneuvered and overpowered them with superior weapons: cunning behavior and rifles and guns. Thus, Africans lost both their young and their old people in that first white-black encounter. Later in history, the scenario repeated itself during their second encounter: the European partition and colonization of African territories.

The second aspect of the slave trade happened because of some West African cosmological beliefs: Ordinarily, persons who committed hideous crimes like murdering a fellow clansman or clanswoman deserved capital punishment, but their Earth-goddess, Ani/Ala (in Igbo), did not permit the spilling of a clansman's or clanswoman's blood. Instead, such criminals were banished to other clans, where they could perform cleansing rites and thereafter lead a normal life again. Also, clansmen or -women who suffered from diseases considered then incurable, including smallpox and dropsy, or kwashiorkor, as well as twins and their mothers, were cast out of their villages to the "evil forests" to prevent them from "infecting" others. The people were treated that way because they were considered abominations to their gods and goddesses. However, some of them who survived in the evil forests wandered off to nearby villages, where they were rehabilitated and adopted as slaves. The young able-bodied men among them worked hard to buy their freedom back, while beautiful and hardworking young women were permitted to marry free men in their adoptive villages. That way, they became free without regard to whatever they were before in their native clans and villages. The rest of the outcasts continued to serve as local slaves until they were sold to the Arabs during the middle passage, or freed whenever they were able to buy their freedom back.

The third category of African slaves were those captured during intertribal wars. Their captors adopted some of them as sons or wives because of their hard work or physical beauty and good manners, which distinguished them from other captives.

In all three scenarios, however, priests and priestesses of the village and clan gods and goddesses were consulted to offer appropriate propitiatory sacrifices before the outcasts and war captives were adopted and integrated into their new clans and villages. Also, in every situation, there was a lot of respect for human blood. Only when the African chiefs and elders became corrupted with European-manufactured goods did they start to sell the people they considered strangers and dregs of society in their midst. The trade in human beings was so lucrative to the white and black partners in crime that African clans and villages were constantly raided for slaves by Europeans and Arabs, who had weapons that Africans could not match; both intruding forces had perfected their crafts during their holy wars: the Crusades and the Jihad. In the end, innocent people became victims.

From the sketchy tale of the slave trade and slave raids, it is easy to imagine the helplessness, agony, and sorrow of the families who could not protect their sons, daughters, mothers, fathers, and cousins against being captured, enslaved, and sent to foreign lands. If such slaves were bought and sold locally, their relatives could visit and sometimes work hard to buy their relatives' freedom. Many family members of those who were taken away became so heartbroken that they suffered heart attacks and mental derangement. In some cases, they committed suicide. Hence, in contemporary American society, Nigerian immigrants, not just African Americans, consider themselves victims of slavery, especially when they recall that those lynched, raped, maimed, and resold from one plantation to another were not Americans but Africans. Besides, during the slave era, one out of every four Africans brought over here in chains was a Nigerian. So it becomes reasonable for people to assume that one in every four African Americans would have been able to trace their roots back to Nigeria, had the slave owners kept the family records of the slaves. Because history has been "whitened," as Malcolm X asserts in his essay, "Learning to Read" (1998, 219–27), it has often been difficult for the younger generations of African Americans to pay enough and serious attention to the African versions of that ugly history, which would have helped to assuage their anger against Nigerian and other African immigrants in the United States.

The most influential factor in the relations between Nigerian Americans and African Americans is the level of education attained. The higher the education, the easier communication becomes. African American civil rights leaders were inspired by the liberation movements in African nation-states to push harder in their struggles to win total sociopolitical freedom from the white-dominated American government. And, as we have seen earlier in this book, Nigerians contributed very much toward the establishment and running of Africana Studies programs, which coincided with the civil rights movements of the 1960s. Simply put, the mutual inspiration that American blacks and African blacks gave each other in the 1960s for their respective liberation movements and struggle enhanced their relations tremendously.

In the entertainment sphere, the collective effort of all Americans of African descent enhanced the relations between Nigerian immigrants and African Americans. The authentic African American songs and music, such as gospel, spirituals, sermons, the blues, jazz, and rap evoked the same kind of emotions that West African High life and Juju music and songs evoked out of the Nigerian immigrants. To them, such African American menu items as chitlins, corn bread, biscuits, chicken, and watermelon compared favorably with the Nigerian pounded yam foofoo, fried chicken, egusi/vegetable soup, and pawpaw, usually served as staples during private and public celebrations. Also in the 1960s and 1970s, the popular TV dance program *Soul Train* gave Nigerian immigrants the opportunity to enjoy themselves the way they did in Nigerian big city nightclubs, in which the music of such artists as I. K. Dairo, King Sunny Ade, Ebenezer Obey, Sonny Okosuns, Stephen Osita Osadebey, Fela Kuti, and Victor Uwaifo were played. Nigerian immigrants' invitations of African Americans to their sociocultural events helped to strengthen their relations.

In other areas, Nigerians tried the Afro hairstyles of African Americans and dreadlocks. African Americans learned to wear and appreciate Nigerian traditional clothing during the occasions in which blacks from the African continent and the Americas came together. In the end, in all those activities, Nigerian and African Americans have been giving each other cultural, emotional, and psychological support, as well as group therapy, which help them to deal with their common minority status in the white-dominated American society.

However, the final factor in the Nigerian–African American intergroup relations is their political ambitions, which is at the moment the weakest and most volatile. Many of the Nigerians who came to the United States beginning from 1925 through the 1980s were not yet immigrants. For that reason, their visa status did not permit them to engage in any political activities in this country. Even after the 1980s, when many of them had become citizens and their American-born children had grown into legal adults, they had not acquired enough of the American political culture to enable them to play politics well. The result of both circumstances was that the Nigerians could not openly support African Americans who sought political offices. Besides, African Americans themselves had not been fully free to seek high political offices before 1965. So neither of the two black groups in the United States had the political clout or wherewithal to support the sociopolitical ambitions of the other until quite recently.

Unaware of the previously mentioned political impediments, some individuals from both groups have often wondered why there has not been effectual political help and support for each group on both the group and individual levels. Nigerian Americans wondered why the black political and civic leaders had not been able to persuade Congress and the various American presidents (except Clinton) to develop foreign policies that would have helped Nigerians as well as other Africans to develop democratic governance that ensure social justice and economic stability for their people. They were disappointed in the African Americans for not doing for Nigeria what Irish Americans, Jewish Americans, and Cuban Americans, for instance, were doing for Ireland, Israel, and Cuba, respectively. On the other hand, African Americans have wondered why Nigerian immigrants did not join in their protest activities and demonstrations, such as those carried out against the physical abuse of Rodney King in Los Angeles as well as some other celebrated cases of police shootings of unarmed African Americans in New Jersey, New York, Cleveland, and Houston. It appears, however, that both groups of black Americans have always been willing to help each other out, but their sociopolitical disability remains a huge obstacle to their giving practical expression to what they feel and hope to do in this area of their intergroup relations.

While the relations of the two groups are generally good and steadily improving on the group level, they seem to be deteriorating on the individual level. To exemplify the deterioration in the interpersonal relations of individuals, two unfortunate incidents can be cited: The first case is about a Nigerian American boy born to an African American mother and a Nigerian American father, which was reported in the news. A twelve-year-old, Prince Nnaedozie

Umegbolu, was made to swallow eighty-seven condoms filled with heroin during his journey from Lagos, Nigeria, to New York. His African American mother, Alissa Walden, said her son was forced to work for Nigerian drug dealers because he was desperate to return to the United States. The boy's Nigerian American father, Chukwunweike Umegbolu, had served seven years of a ten-year sentence for his role in a heroin ring that trafficked more than $33 million into Atlanta (http://www.usafricaonline.com/drugs.umegbolu.html, accessed May 20, 2002).

The boy's mother permitted her son to visit his paternal grandparents in Nigeria, even though she was divorced from her son's father. The grandparents did not protect their grandson from being used by drug traffickers whom he had he approached for money to buy a return ticket from Lagos, Nigeria, to Atlanta, Georgia.

Another case involved a Nigerian American high-school boy, who was stabbed to death in Hartford, Connecticut, in 1993. Although he was bright and at the top of his class, his classmates made fun of his Nigerian accent. One day, after classes, one of the African American students accosted him and blocked his way out of the school. Then the Nigerian American boy attempted to push the other out of his way, and they began to fight. During their fight, the African American boy was given a knife by other African American boys, which he used to stab the Nigerian American boy to death.

Both of these two select cases were so devastating to the victims and their parents that their ripple effects on the Nigerian–African American relations created temporary stereotyping of one group by the other, as well as intraracist remarks that nearly divided the black community in the given towns and neighborhoods. But both sentiments were promptly suppressed by the civic leaders of both black ethnic groups.

In spite of the strained relations of Nigerian immigrants and African Americans on the personal level, their overall intergroup relations on the group level is very good at the moment. Both groups are becoming increasingly aware of their rights and responsibilities and are addressing the sociopolitical and economic disadvantages vis-à-vis their minority status in this white-dominated society. The awareness derives from Nigerian immigrants' decision to settle permanently in the United States and their adjustment to all aspects of the American national life, including how to bond with people whose racial, social, political, and economic destiny they share. African Americans have come to learn that continental Africa is not as "dark" as it was portrayed earlier to them by white colonialist-cum-racist writers on Africa. With that awareness and enlightenment, they have begun to accept with pride their

Africanness, unlike in the past, when some of them were ashamed of their African heritage and peoples.

RELATIONS WITH OTHER AFRICAN IMMIGRANTS

The African immigrants that Nigerian immigrants associate closely with in the United States are those from sub-Saharan African countries also known as Black Africa. Although most of them look alike to non-Africans, the Africans themselves do recognize the differences between them, in terms of physical features and cultural differences, especially in areas like ethnicity, religion, language, and sociopolitical views. Most of the differences are predicated upon the various peoples' colonial experiences, belief systems, and world-views. In the West African subregion, for instance, the communities are sub-divided into two groups: those who were once colonized by Britain and are English-speaking, and those who were once colonized by France and are French-speaking. The difference between the British and French colonial systems of government shaped the sociopolitical and cultural views of each of the former colonial blocs.

In the English-speaking group, to which Nigeria belongs, the West African peoples assumed responsibility for their own destiny upon attainment of independence, a process that implied regaining their precolonial sovereignty. And with that sovereignty, they had the option of maintaining or withdrawing their membership in the Commonwealth of Nations, which is an organization of former British colonies. Before independence, the organization was called the British Commonwealth under Queen Elizabeth II of Britain. Currently, all heads of the member states of the organization are called Commonwealth heads of government, and they share equality with the British head of government. The administrative head of the organization is the commonwealth Secretary-General, who can be elected from any of the member states. A Nigerian, Chief Emeka Anyaoku, became the first African and the third person to be elected into that high office.

On the other hand, the French-speaking countries were slower in pursuing their political independence because of the French political system, which made the indigenous people of the African countries they colonized somehow subservient to the French people. This is because the French preached the message that their civilization, *la çivilization haute,* was superior to the African, which they said must evolve from the subhuman level to the French level. The inhabitants of the French-speaking countries bought into that colonial mentality and thus preferred evolution to revolution as a means of reaching that level. Those who received their French education and embraced the French culture and civilization became *les évolués* (the evolved). They could then live in France, become French citizens, and belong to the French parliament. An example of the evolved persons is the former President of Senegal, Monsieur Léopold Sédar Senghor, who lived in Paris and married a Parisian woman.

From this simple illustration of the different sociopolitical mentalities of the West African peoples, it is easy to surmise the kind of differences there are between sub-Saharan African peoples who were once ruled by the British, the French, the Germans, the Portuguese, and the Spanish. Suffice it to say that the sociopolitical ideologies the African peoples absorbed from their erstwhile colonial masters went a long way in putting a knife on those ropes of culture and civilization that once bound precolonial Africa together.

All through the African peoples' struggles against European colonial powers for political independence, Nigeria played a leading role in the formation of the sociopolitical and economic organization known as Organization of African Unity (OAU). And after the attainment of political independence by all West African countries, Nigeria played another leading role in the formation of an economic organization for the subregion known as Economic Community of West African States (ECOWAS), which brings the English-speaking and French-speaking communities together. Founded in Lagos, Nigeria, on May 28, 1975, and composed of fifteen member states, ECOWAS has its headquarters in Abuja, the new federal capital of Nigeria.

Aware and conscious of Nigeria's leadership roles in continental Africa, Nigerian immigrants have been striving to play the same leadership roles among Africans in the United States. They use their numerical strength, academic and professional excellence, and material wealth (some of which advantages they share with Ghanaians) to lead.

On the sociocultural and political levels, Nigerian immigrants work hand-in-hand with the Nigerian diplomatic mission in the United States to promote African interests. They did so when Africans campaigned for the election and reelection of Kofi A. Annan of Ghana as the first black African to serve as Secretary-General of the United Nations in January 1997 and January 2001, respectively. In return, other African immigrants lobbied their native countries' diplomatic missions to support the appointments of Nigerians to the membership and chairmanship of powerful committees of the world body. And because of the leadership roles of Nigerian immigrants in forging black African solidarity in the United States, the American Congress and the United Nations have started to pay greater attention to the sociopolitical and economic needs of the peoples of Africa.

In essence, Nigerian immigrants' relations with other immigrant groups from Africa is very cordial. Evidence of the good relations among the black African immigrant groups can be found in how all cheered the Nigerian Super Eagles to victory in the 1994 FIFA (Soccer) World Cup championship games. Similarly, they all rallied together with African Americans to protest a gory incident in which Amadou Diallo, a West African immigrant, was shot forty-one times and killed by four New York police officers on February 4, 1999. Although not all American blacks in similar instances got the justice they sought from the court system, the protests they staged in response to such incidents helped to bring all of them together and to create the need for close intergroup relations among them. In the short term, the protests raised their sociopolitical consciousness and sense of responsibility to a higher level.

Finally, the longer the Nigerian immigrants stay in the United States, the clearer they see the need to develop smooth and healthy intergroup relations with all other Americans. Also, because the poor social, political, and economic problems of their native Nigeria have forced many of them to make the awesome decision to settle permanently, some of them have learned to stoically engage in adjustment and adaptation processes that should enhance and quicken the pace of their intergroup relations with other Americans. So far, all the effort they have made in that direction seems to augur well for their mutual coexistence with the rest of American peoples.

7

Evolving Nigerian American Identity: Impediments, Legacy, and Hope

From the late 1960s, Nigerians have dispersed to all parts of the world, especially the United States and Great Britain. Ironically, ugly historic world events, such as the slave trade and colonialism, which the black world justifiably bemoans, are the very events that, in an indirect way, encouraged many Nigerians to emigrate to other countries where they now live, study, work, and do business. For without the two events, prehistoric African territories, once closed societies, could not have been opened up for international business, trade, education, and sociopolitical intercourse; without colonization, Nigerians could not have received Western education and the English language, which make international communication and exchange of ideas possible; and, without the intercultural rapport with the various "conquering" and "civilizing" powers that Nigerians came in contact with all through their colonial and postcolonial experiences with the West, their social culture (as it now stands) may not have been modified in ways that made it viable enough to compete with other international cultures. In essence, what Nigerians and other sub-Saharan Africans lost to slavery and colonialism—their dignity and sovereignty—have been gradually reclaimed in contemporary black societies. And it is those historical encounters between Nigerians and the West, when they were still in Nigeria, that prepared them as immigrants in the United States to compete favorably with other immigrants.

To exemplify the unintended benefits of slavery and colonialism that people generally overlook, it should be noted that the first person to put into print Nigerian culture, customs, and traditions was Olaudah Equiano, a Nigerian slave from Igboland. He was sold into slavery in Barbados, West

Indies, where he worked hard to buy his freedom back, and from there he emigrated to England. While in England, Equiano received adequate Western education to enable him to write the first slave narrative in the world, titled *The Interesting Narrative of the Life of Olaudah Equiano or Gustavus Vassa, the African, Written by Himself* (1789). In it, Equiano not only exposed the miserable and inhuman conditions of African slaves in Europe and the Caribbean but also painted a vivid picture of his native Igbo country and its people, customs, and traditions, which contrasted sharply with those painted about Africa in general as the dark continent by colonialists, who wrote out of the cursory observations of the peoples and their cultures, customs, and civilizations they made while serving as European administrators, explorers, and sailors in that part of the world.

The book, dedicated to "the Lords Spiritual and Temporal, and the Commons of the Parliament of Great Britain" on March 24, 1789, went a long way to influence the votes that that parliament cast to abolish slave trade in 1803, for Equiano had prayed the august body to

> [p]ermit me, with the greatest deference and respect, to lay at your feet the following genuine narrative, the chief design of which is to excite in your august assemblies a sense of compassion for the miseries which the Slave-Trade has entailed on my unfortunate countrymen. By the horrors of that trade was I first torn away from all the tender connections that were naturally dear to my heart; but these, through the mysterious ways of Providence, I ought to regard as infinitely more than compensated by the introduction I have thence obtained to the knowledge of the Christian religion, and of a nation which, by its liberal sentiments, its humanity, the glorious freedom of its government, and its proficiency in arts and sciences, has exalted the dignity of human nature. (Equiano 1814, 3)

Because of the book's impact on the British Parliament and people, as well as the abolitionist movements in Europe and the United States, the black world (which had hitherto depended wholly on oral communications) saw for the first time the power of the written word and rhetoric. It served as a long lasting Nigerian literary legacy to the black world: Frederick Douglass, an ex-slave and American abolitionist, read Equiano's slave narrative and was influenced and inspired to write his own narrative, titled *Narrative of the Life of Frederick Douglass, an African Slave* (1845). It had a similar but not comparable impact on the American Congress and people. But it contributed significantly to the signing of the Emancipation Proclamation of 1863, which made slavery illegal in the southern parts of the United States. Other classic slave narratives that were inspired by the Nigerian author's narrative include *The History of Mary Prince, A West Indian Slave* (1831), and Harriet Jacobs's *Incidents in the Life of a Slave Girl* (1861). All of them together sowed the seeds of freedom and unity for black peoples of the Americas.

Nearly two hundred years after the publication of Equiano's book, which exposed the evil effects of slavery, another Nigerian young man also from Igboland, Chinua Achebe, published his first novel, *Things Fall Apart* (1958), which exposed the evil effects of colonialism on the colonized peoples of Africa. In that novel, Achebe made use of elements common in European and American fiction—plot/structure, point of view, figurative language, tone and voice, setting, characters, and symbols and imagery—to convey its theme. However, the local color—the unique quality of Africanness Achebe gave those elements—made the novel a hybrid genre: African writers and readers have since validated its story and verbal art, setting, cultural context, characters, and overall theme as authentically African. In effect, the style and content of *Things Fall Apart* triggered and helped to establish what can be called the Achebe school of writers and the Achebe tradition in African fiction, the great literature with the power to dispel European-manufactured myths about African cultures, providing readers, native and foreign, with insiders' perspectives on African cultures and civilizations.

Since 1990, Chinua Achebe has been teaching at Bard College in New York, where he serves as professor of English and African literary and cultural studies. His published works, as well as those of Wole Soyinka (a Nigerian) and Ngugi wa Thiong'o (a Kenyan), have combined with the writings of such modern African American authors as Toni Morrison, Maya Angelou, Richard Wright, Ralph Ellison, and James Baldwin to give black or Africana literature a deserved spotlight in the canon of world literature. Also, beginning from the Harlem Renaissance, the black writers have continued to use their works to revamp and disseminate the Africana cultures and civilizations that went underground following the onslaught of the slave trade, slavery, and colonialism, which victimized the black world collectively.

Like Equiano and Achebe, contemporary Nigerian writers in diaspora have been using their writings as forums from where they can criticize the ills of their societies and suggest ways of bringing about healthy changes or ideas to improve the lives and fortunes of the people. From that point of view, such writers can be called social critics and their works *protest* writing. And it is that kind of writing in the areas of literature, political science, sociology, ethnography, and history that has liberated black people from the slave and colonial mentality, and rekindled pride in the collective psyche of the black world. The writers of the Harlem Renaissance started that process of decolonizing the collective black mind in the United States. For that reason, some people believe that the fight against sociopolitical and economic woes of Nigerians in diaspora could be led by committed Nigerian immigrants in the United States.

Wole Soyinka, another Nigerian although of Yoruba extraction, who lives in Atlanta and teaches at Emory University, is an extremely politically committed Nigerian writer. Right from the days of the Nigerian civil war, when he was jailed for criticizing the way the military waged the war against Biafrans, he has written as a social critic and taken part in physical demonstrations in Nigeria and the United States against civil rights abuse. The Nobel Prize for literature that he won in 1986 attests to the high quality of his writings, and the themes of civil rights, equality, and social justice they embody are the hallmarks of his career as a committed literary artist and sociopolitical activist. Without his relentless devotion to both aspects of his career, Nigeria could not have transformed into the political democracy it is today; at least, not at the time it did in 1999. Although he is a permanent resident in the United States, he frequently goes back to troubleshoot whenever and wherever his help is needed in Nigeria. This is why, unlike most Nigerians resident in the United States, Soyinka refuses to become a dual citizen.

For contemporary Nigerian immigrants in the United States, their identity issue is of critical importance. We have already seen earlier in this book how difficult it was for many of them to make the decision to settle permanently in the United States—a decision that seemed to them as being tantamount to abandoning their country, their people, their ancestors, and their culture. Those who could not deal with it had to return home, while the others who wanted to stay (no matter how painful it was for them to do so) took one of two options: to become permanent residents and go back to Nigeria as visitors whenever they wanted, or to become dual citizens.

In taking either of the two options, Nigerian immigrants invoked the spirit and help of their ancestors (dead or living), whose dedicated services to their native Nigerian and community causes became models that latter generations of Nigerians abroad could emulate. Here lies the importance of the examples set by Equiano and Achebe. Equiano's example teaches that although he was sold into Western slavery by his own people, he used what he learned in slavery—literacy and writing—to explain his people, their culture, and their civilization to the reading world. Neither the enslavement of Equiano nor his righteous anger against those who colluded with white slave traders to sell him prevented him from doing a humanitarian duty by his fellow ex-slaves and serving slaves, or from becoming an indirect literary representative of his native Nigeria, which he had lost as a result of being made a slave in a foreign country. Instead, he overcame evil with goodness—a remarkable demonstration of both altruism and patriotism.

Achebe played the role of bringing literary independence to continental Africa as well as engaging in continued fight against political corruption and civil rights abuse in Nigeria, even as he currently lives and works in the United States. From what people know about him, he would have been the last person to remain in this country as long as he has done. But he is here because he was involved in an automobile accident that left him paralyzed. Fortunately for the Igbo and Nigeria in particular, and the reading world in general, he did not die. He also had the good fortune of being hired and housed by Bard College. There Achebe has continued to demonstrate practically his contention that "to redress the inequities of global oppression, writers must focus on where they come from, insisting that their value systems are as legitimate as any other. He asserts that stories are a real source of power in the world and that to imitate the literature of another culture is to give that power away" (Achebe 2000, dust jacket). He gives lectures and grants interviews on African literary and cultural studies in major American colleges and universities, interweaving their themes with other subjects, such as human rights abuse, the development of political democracy, and empowerment of certain marginalized ethnic groups by the ruling elite, whenever he occasionally travels to Nigeria. He does all that in spite of the physical disability he lives with, because of his dogged determination to serve his beloved country and continent with all his might, even from a long distance, and because of his family that surrounds him with enviable love.

FACTORS THAT AFFECT THE DEVELOPING OF TRUE NIGERIAN AND NIGERIAN AMERICAN IDENTITY

Many factors militate against the development of true Nigerian identity whether at home in Nigeria or here in the United States. The first and foremost of the factors is *ethnocentrism,* which the British commonly referred to as "tribalism" when they ruled Nigeria. Another factor is the wounds of the Nigeria-Biafra War, which have not fully healed even though the war ended more than three decades ago. The third factor is the military dictatorships of the postwar Nigeria. And the fourth is the unsatisfied yearnings of Nigerians everywhere for true democratic dispensation in their native country. All of these factors have a bearing on the way they relate to each other on both the group and individual levels. However, against these unfavorable factors in the evolving Nigerian identity is the positive influence of Nigerian Americans on the geopolitical and socioeconomic conditions in twenty-first-century Nigeria.

The Role of Ethnocentrism

As we saw in Chapter 1, Great Britain began in the late 1800s the formal process of creating Nigeria as a country by lumping together many West African territories and peoples whose customs, cultures, and traditions were in many ways diverse and conflicting. Although the people resisted being yoked together by the alien authority, they were forced to become a country in 1914 because the British had the superior power of the guns and cannons and cunning diplomacy. In the absence of such essential and cohesive factors as common religion, worldview, language, and culture, which bind people together, the only force that brought them together was coercive British presence and rule in the ill-fated country. So, instead of developing the love of one's country—patriotism—Nigerians developed the love of one's ethnic group—ethnocentrism. The British government and agencies in Nigeria then did not mind that, as long as they were able to cart away as much of Nigeria's natural and human resources as they could from 1900 until 1960, when the people, led by political leaders of the three regions—Dr. Nnamdi Azikiwe from the East, Alhaji Tafawa Balewa from the North, and Chief Obafemi Awolowo from the West—became politically independent of Great Britain. But once the British colonial masters left, the ethnic sentiments, which they had managed to relegate to the background during the colonial days resurfaced with a vengeance in postcolonial Nigeria and remained prevalent until the outbreak of the civil war.

The Wounds of the Nigeria-Biafra War

Although the Nigeria-Biafra War ended in the defeat of the Biafrans, the then military head of state, General Yakubu Gowon, was very anxious to reunite Nigeria as quickly as possible. So, while receiving the formal Biafran surrender documents from General Effiong, he declared on January 15, 1970, that there were "no victors, no vanquished." In addition, he decreed in a catchy slogan, "Reconciliation, Reintegration, and Reconstruction," that the surrendering Biafran armed forces and their people would not face any form of reprisals from Nigerian armed forces. But as it soon turned out, Gowon made the two pronouncements as a clever way of dissuading the ex-Biafrans from emigrating from Nigeria to form a government-in-exile with their popular leader, Chukwuemeka Odumegwu-Ojukwu, General of the People's Army, who had just gone into exile in a West African country, Gabon, a few days before the Biafran surrender.

The war left gaping wounds in the bodies, minds, and souls of Nigerians of all ethnic extractions, for there were heavy casualties on both sides of the conflicts. With the Igbo—leaders of the Biafran cause and one of the so-called Nigerian sociopolitical tripod (Igbo, Hausa, Yoruba)—humiliated and taken out of the sociopolitical equation, the victorious Northern military leaders took over the reins of government. And there were no serious efforts to reconcile, reintegrate, and rehabilitate all those maimed and disenfranchised by the civil war. The people became disillusioned, and yearned for the still-born Biafra, "the land of the rising sun." They remained Nigerians in name but Biafrans in spirit. Thus their sociopolitical and economic conditions, coupled with their ethnocentric fervor, made it most unlikely for many Easterners to develop a true Nigerian national identity within and outside that country.

The Role of Military Dictatorships

From January 15, 1970, when the civil war ended, to May 29, 1999, when Nigeria began once again to experiment on democracy under a civilian administration, no fewer than seven warlords ruled Nigeria: General Yakubu Gowon (1966–75), General Murtala Mohammed (1975–76), General Olusegun Obasanjo (1976–79), Major-General Muhamadu Buhari (1983–85), General Ibrahim Babangida (1985–93), General Sani Abacha (1993–98), and General Abdulsalaam Abubakar (1998–99). The only civilian interregnum occurred between 1979 and 1983, when Alhaji Shehu Shagari (a Northerner) won elections to become the first postwar civilian president, only to be toppled by Major-General Buhari in a 1983 military coup. The other brief civilian regime, which was headed by Chief Ernest Shonekan, lasted four months: from August to November 1993, when it was toppled by General Abacha in another military coup. So, for three long decades (1970–99), Nigeria was ruled by military juntas, except for the four and one-third years they allowed civilians to rule under their watchful eyes. For all those long years, Nigeria felt like a military camp because of the ubiquitous presence of the military people among civilians.

Apart from the obvious evils of the dictatorial regimes, such as lack of fundamental human rights, absence of the rule of law, general corruption, and debauchery, the country was torn into two parts—Northern Nigeria and Southern Nigeria—instead of the four regions into which it was divided before the war—Eastern Nigeria, Midwestern Nigeria, Northern Nigeria, and Western Nigeria. Also, because six of the seven warlords came from the North and the remaining one from the West, the governance of the country was usually in the hands of Northern military rulers and their civilian cronies. Consequently, unqualified Hausa/Fulani military personnel, civil servants, educators, and diplomats were automatically promoted and appointed to head military and government institutions and agencies. The federal capital of Nigeria was moved from Lagos in the South to Abuja in the North, and most of the ambassadorial appointments went to inexperienced Hausa/Fulani people, except for a few Yoruba people who were appointed because of the influence of General Obasanjo and other Yoruba senior military officers.

The military appointed heads of federal universities and colleges instead of allowing such appointments to be made by academic institutions, which would have used standard procedures and criteria to do so. The laws of the land were replaced with military decrees, and social amenities, such as piped water, good roads, electricity, hospitals, and medical supplies became scarce or nonexistent in virtually all parts of the country except in the North.

Eventually, civil unrest, as well as ethnic and religious tensions, was felt everywhere in the country. The military commanders ordered soldiers to deal with the situation, which they saw as a threat to their very existence. And before the civilians knew what was happening, the soldiers had a field day killing and maiming unarmed civilians, especially those who took part in legitimate demonstrations against military decrees that the people felt were against them. In the end, highly trained professors, technocrats, and other professionals from Eastern, Midwestern, and Western Nigeria left the country in droves to find jobs in foreign countries, thus creating a phenomenon the government dubbed "brain drain." In the end, all the major ethnic groups developed deep and far-reaching mutual suspicions for one another, which have continued to make it almost impossible for Nigerians in diaspora to develop enviable Nigerian identity and patriotism.

Unsatisfied Yearnings for Democratic Dispensation

In this information age, events in any part of the world are easily transmitted to the rest of the world through cable television networks, e-mail, the telephone, faxes, and other satellite systems. That means, with regard to the Nigerian situations, Nigerian immigrants could learn of what went on in their native country instantly and communicate easily with their relatives through any of those means. Besides, they could fly in and out of Nigeria for business or for pleasure whenever they pleased. Also, the use of cell phones and computers became a common practice, which has enhanced business and interpersonal communications between the people inside and outside the country.

Yet, in spite of such easy communication links between Nigerians at home and those abroad, all was not well with the country. The people fought hard to bring in a democratically elected administration in 1999, but they were yet to experience the benefits of democracy. That is because there still existed a lot of nagging sociopolitical, economic, and religious problems—a situation that bothered everybody, including Nigerian elected office holders. For instance, in the Reverend Samuel Odunaike Memorial Lecture 2002 held at Ikeja, Lagos, on June 21, 2002, the Nigerian senate president, Anyim Pius Anyim, was quoted as saying that "the nation's persistent sociopolitical instability was traceable to tribal-cum-regional politics, religious bigotry, political violence, farce political rivalry, leadership without commitment to the people, fear of domination, and corruption" (http://www.ngrguardiannews.com/news/ articles, accessed June 22, 2002).

In the United States, Nigerian immigrants saw and heard of the social unrest and the destruction of human lives and property in all parts of Nigeria. They found that religious uprisings became more complex: As the population of Northern Christians rapidly increased, the Islamic fundamentalists became more angry and so attacked the Christians. However, whenever there was an outbreak of religious hostilities, Northern Christians teamed up with Southerners to fight the Muslims. And whenever an attack of Christians took place in the north, Southern Christians attacked Muslims and Hausas in the south. That is the "tribal-cum-regional politics and religious bigotry" the Nigerian senate president was referring to, which characterized the Obasanjo administration. Because there are no winners but losers all around in such conflicts, many people blamed Obasanjo for not being able to control the situation. Also, they saw him as a puppet to Northern military men like General Ibrahim Babangida, who reportedly financed his election into office, and General Theophilus Danjuma, who reportedly masterminded and executed the 1967 coup that took the lives of the head of the Nigerian military government from the East, General Aguiyi-Ironsi, and the military governor of Western Nigeria, Colonel Adekunle Fajuyi, and paved the way for the Hausa/Fulani military oligarchy that followed. General Danjuma was very old in 1999, and yet President Obasanjo appointed him minister of defense to keep the Northerners happy. That seems to explain why there were no security or law and order in that country during the first Obasanjo administration. And that may also explain the people's constant yearning for true democracy that has remained unsatisfied, in spite of Obasanjo's democratic election into the high office by the people. Furthermore, the people were so disillusioned in 2002 that they clamored to form new political parties, to challenge Obasanjo's ruling party, the Peoples Democratic Party, in the 2003 presidential elections. And some of those clamoring for new parties or the merger of old ones came from the PDP. What came out of all the political maneuvering and gamesmanship that went on in 2002 was that Obasanjo was reelected president in the Nigerian general elections that took place in April 2003.

Before then, however, professional politicians came to the United States for consultations with Nigerian Americans, who gave them political advice, money, and gifts, such as computers, cell phones, typewriters, and copier machines to equip their political offices, ready for the elections. The political activities were so heated up among Nigerian Americans of South East and South South Nigerian descent because they felt that their people were marginalized by Northern and Western political and military heavyweights. Nevertheless, with the power of incumbency, rigging, and lots of money, Obasanjo and his PDP party retained power the second time around.

The Construction of Nigerian American Identity

Here in the United States, Nigerian immigrants have been dealing with the question of their identity for a while. In their national, state, and ethnic organizations, in Internet publications, as well as in their lifestyle, they have been making a concerted effort to create an identity that is separate from that of African Americans or those of other African immigrants in the United States. They do so with the knowledge that without coming together as a people to face their common lot and destiny in a society where all black peoples are classified as one people, they could easily lose their individual ethnic heritage and identity. However, following the continual sociopolitical and ethnoreligious upheavals in their native Nigeria, many of the immigrants became easily disenchanted with the prospect of making a committed effort toward the construction of a Nigerian identity at home and abroad. But because no people can escape their common identity and destiny, Nigerian immigrants must do certain things to create and maintain a viable group identity they can call their own in this pluralistic American society, including confronting their past history, which includes their colonial history and education, interethnic trade and business, and interethnic marriages, whose lessons could help them deal with their present sociopolitical and economic predicament.

Colonial History. When the British were still in Nigeria, they learned to rule it as though they were dealing with two separate nations: the Islamic North and the Christian South. While they ruled the Southern parts of the country directly, they introduced a system of government they called Indirect Rule in the North, which enabled them to use Islamic scholars and indigenous elders to deal with the people because their indigenous culture and customs were intertwined with Islam. As a result of the differences in the customs and cultures of the two parts of the country, Nigeria could not speak with one voice at first, with regard to getting political independence from

Britain in 1957, when they had hoped to get it alongside Gold Coast, which became Ghana that year. When the two Southern sections of the country (East and West) pressed hard for it, the North said they were not ready. However, by way of comprise, all three parts reached an accord with Great Britain to attain the status of Self-Rule, instead of independence, in 1957.

Despite the leadership role Dr. Nnamdi Azikiwe (who came from the East) played in the Nigerian constitutional talks with the British in London, back home in Nigeria, a Northerner, Alhaji Tafawa Balewa, was elected the prime minister, and he served Nigeria in that capacity from 1957 until 1966, when he was killed in that country's first military coup. At any rate, Dr. Azikiwe became the first indigenous Governor-General in 1960, when Nigeria attained its independence status, and president in 1963, when it became a republic.

The lesson to learn from this historical fact is that after the initial disagreement the North and the South had in 1957, their political leaders ultimately made some concerted effort that won the people the independence they craved. Also, of the three political leaders representing Eastern, Northern, and Western regions, Balewa had the least formal education; yet, because the people spoke through the ballot and not the bullet, he became the leader of government rather than Azikiwe, who had the highest educational qualification, particularly in political science, which earned him the accolades "Father of Modern Nigeria" and "Zik of Africa." Chief Obafemi Awolowo from the West, who was also politically savvy and well educated, could not win either the prime minister position or that of Governor-General, so he settled for the position of premier of Western Nigeria. Even after the war, when he vied for the position of president of Nigeria, he lost again, and he died shortly after. But he had done much that contributed to the building of Nigeria as an independent nation.

In all the Nigerian national elections, Northerners voted as one unit for Northern candidates, whereas Southerners voted as two units for Eastern and Western candidates; later in 1962, when the Midwest region was carved out of the West, the South voted as three units. All that gave the North numerical advantage over the South in their voting bids. The situation became worse when the military governments divided the country into thirty-six states, and arbitrarily so in favor of the Hausa/Fulani and Yoruba ethnic groups. Although the third leg of the tripod, the Igbo, claimed to be as many in number as each of the other two ethnic groups, they were given fewer states than the Hausa/Fulani and the Yoruba peoples. Other ethnic groups also felt that they were marginalized—a feeling that they have continued to express since the military era.

Ignorance of Their Sociocultural History. One cause of the sociopolitical upheavals and ethnocentric prejudice in Nigeria is the people's ignorance of their collective sociocultural history. Many of them do not realize that what unites them as a people is more than what has been dividing them:

Education. The Southerners have been at the vanguard of educational development in Nigeria, beginning from the precolonial days, when the Christian missionaries introduced churches and schools into the country. The Yoruba, the Ijaw, the Efik, and the Igbo who live on the coastal lines of Nigeria embraced Western education and culture before the Northern peoples of Nigeria, who embraced Islamic studies and culture, which were in conflict with the Western system; but as a result of the educational services that Southerners rendered to them, all parts of the country ultimately embraced Western education. Also, the returnee slaves from England to Sierra Leone and those from the United States to Liberia were primarily from the Southern region of Nigeria.

Western education, more than politics, brought Nigerians together more. For example, not many Nigerians know that the Reverend J. C. Taylor, a native of Freetown, Sierra Leone, whose parents were born in Igboland, was one of the early missionaries to Onitsha. And when he needed to deepen his knowledge of Igbo language, he went to England to understudy the Reverend J. F. Schön, a renowned German linguist. Furthermore, the earliest dictionary of the Igbo language, published in 1882, was produced by the Yoruba ex-slave turned scholar and missionary, the Reverend Samuel Adjai Crowther. Also, many Hausa, Ijaw, and Nupe people may not have known that Crowther also studied their languages, which helped the early missionaries in Nigeria, under Schön, to translate the Bible into many Nigerian languages. Those early Nigerian missionaries used education to unite the ethnic peoples of Nigeria.

When Nigeria became a British colony, the missionaries hired Southerners, especially the Igbo, to go and teach students in their schools all over the country. Their services were very much needed in the North, where the indigenous Islamic scholars could not provide Western education for their people. And when it became a British government policy that every child in Nigeria should receive at least an elementary school education, those who were trained and sent to teach in those schools were Southern teachers. Even though Northerners initially resisted Western education, the Southern teachers persuaded many parents to see their point of view on that issue. The Northern elders were happy to live with Igbo people as welcome neighbors.

Interethnic Trade and Business. Although people regard the Igbo as the most enterprising ethnic group in prewar Nigeria, the Hausa/Fulani were also enterprising in their own way. For while the Igbo went to all nooks and corners doing one form of trade business or another with the indigenous people and British companies, the Hausa/Fulani were seen in many Nigerian townships selling kola nuts and cows (which have always been the principal source of meat supply in Nigeria). In time, the Igbo became merchants of foreign goods and local agricultural products, and transporters. They could do so because of their early acquisition of Western education and entrepreneurial spirit, which enabled them to understand basic economic principles and market economy that gave them some advantage over Northern nomadic, subsistence farmers. But, in time, they recruited and trained the Hausa/Fulani people as middlemen and clerks. And when many Northerners received Western education, they evolved into business partners with the Igbo. Today many of them have become business tycoons.

Other ethnic peoples of Southern Nigeria were, and still are, as highly educated and enterprising as the Igbo, but they remained, in the main, regional businesspeople. For instance, the Yoruba stayed in their native Western Nigeria, especially in Lagos, the former capital of Nigeria, to work with foreign companies, while others worked in their village markets. However, not many of them worked in the private sector outside their region. The Efik, the Ijaw, the Urhobo, and the Ibibio did the same, especially in Calabar, Port Harcourt, Benin, Asaba, Uyo, and Ikot Ekpene, respectively. The less formal education they had, the more they remained in their villages to engage in subsistence farming and petty training. The Igbo did all that in their own villages but penetrated other people's territories for more trade business. In fact, they developed everywhere they lived, as they made it their second home. They lived in peace with their "landlords" until the war pushed them back to Igboland. But despite the vagaries of that war, many of them went back to all parts of Nigeria after the war. That move has continued to create ethnic tensions in the face of the high unemployment figures in contemporary Nigeria.

The Igbo needed the people among whom they lived and did business before and after the war as business partners and consumers of their products and services. Consequently, the Igbo have remained constant in serving as the only ethnic group that has always united all the other ethnic groups, because of their presence everywhere in Nigeria. But the propaganda mounted against them—being accused of ethnic bigotry and domination—became one of the causes of the civil war that nearly exterminated them as a people. Their legacy of hard work and self-reliance has continued to benefit the rest of postwar Nigeria.

Interethnic Marriages. One of the most significant but often underrated unifying factors in Nigerian national life is interethnic marriage. Before the civil war, some Igbo men in virtually all parts of Nigeria were interested in marrying women who lived near them. The result was the births of great Nigerians of interethnic marriages. For example, among such bi-ethnic children are General Ike Nwachukwu, whose father was Igbo and mother was Hausa, the Nigerian legal luminary and first attorney-general of Imo State, Barrister Kalu

Kalu Ogba, whose father was Igbo and mother was Efik, and the political leader of the Action Group, Mazi S. G. Ikoku, whose father was Igbo and mother was Ibibio. Furthermore, the most revered and beloved Igbo leader and one-time president of the World Council of Churches, Ezeogo Akanu Ibiam, was married to a Yoruba woman, and the renowned Igbo novelist and one-time registrar of the West African Examinations Council, Chukwuemeka Ike, married a Yoruba woman.

Furthermore, Nigerian men and women of Biafran extraction living in the United States during the war fell in love and got married with Nigerian Americans of different ethnic backgrounds. At the end of the war, five out of the then twelve Nigerian state military governors married Igbo women. There were similar interethnic marriages between other Nigerian ethnic peoples.

Through those marriages, Nigerians gradually learned to live together as a people, resulting in the puncturing of the self-mystique of ethnic bigotry of some, while raising the low self-esteem of others. The positive development became a trend in the marriage institution of Nigerians, assisted by the transformation that took place in the people's academic, religious, social, political, and economic lives. Specifically for Nigerian immigrants in the United States, distance played a major role in their marriages. Some of them, who got married before coming to the United States, could not bring their spouses over as soon as they wanted. So they had to wait until they got their green card or became citizens through the naturalization process. For the unmarried ones among them, the next best thing for them to do was to marry fellow Nigerians of different ethnic backgrounds. Besides, some of the marriages that parents and other relatives used to arrange for their children became unacceptable to the younger but highly educated generation of Nigerians, whose new land and its cultural norms and mores could not tolerate arranged or long-distance marriage pacts.

Essentially, interethnic marriages, especially those enjoyed by Nigerian Americans, have begun to break down the barriers of ethnic bigotry, even primacy, that breeds disunity among Nigerian ethnic peoples, which the immigrants brought with them to the United States.

To summarize, Nigerian Americans are socially conscious of the violence, starvation, and lack of social justice occurring every day in their native Nigerian communities. Above all, many are disturbed by the absence of true democracy in that country, even after it had emerged from a bloody civil war and the subsequent military juntas that ruled it until a civilian regime was elected in 1999, with the assistance of the United States. For that reason, Nigerian Americans have been seeking ways of changing the situation for the good of all Nigerians at home and abroad.

PART IV

CONCLUSION

8

The Impact of Nigerian Americans on American Society

Nigerians in the United States began making their contributions to the American society as soon as they came to the United States as scholars and graduate students in the 1960s. However, after their civil war, more and more Nigerians came and later made the awesome decision to become immigrants—a decision that was facilitated by their prior knowledge of the English language and by the dual citizenship granted to them by the United States and Nigerian governments. In fact, the knowledge of English they had before coming made it a lot easier for them to adapt more rapidly to American educational, economic, and religious institutions, which enhanced tremendously their chances of becoming citizens through the naturalization process. Also, while it was difficult for many of them to undergo the necessary sociocultural and educational changes in their new society, their competitive, frontier spirit buoyed them up to face courageously whatever challenges came their way. They saw becoming citizens as opportunity, challenge, and service.

So far, the services that Nigerian Americans render to the American society are not well-known to either the "New Americans" or to the "Old Americans," who came primarily from Europe, because the Nigerians themselves have not acted as one united immigrant group. Also, the impact of their services has been determined essentially by their peculiar patterns of adaptation in the United States: they came initially to receive American higher education, make as much money as they could, and go back to live in Nigeria, until the poor sociopolitical and economic conditions there forced them to come back and live permanently in the United States. Hence, as a new immigrant group, they seemed always to be in a state of flux.

As individuals, the Nigerian immigrants have been making invaluable contributions, which have earned them accolades, honors, and recognition. But the contributions do not have as much traction or weight as they would have had if they were collective contributions of a group, and their impact would have been felt or recognized by other American ethnic nationalities. Instead, their ethnic division continues to prevent them from coming together as Nigerian Americans to represent their achievements as a collective contribution to their new nation.

This chapter describes briefly some of the major contributions of Nigerian Americans and their impact on various areas of American national life and professional activity.

EDUCATION AND PROFESSIONAL SERVICE

There are more than ten thousand Nigerian American professors serving in American universities and colleges, the majority of them in humanities and the social sciences. But with the inroads they have made in the study of the natural sciences and technology and in medicine, a significant number of Nigerian Americans also serve as professors, research assistants, and lab technicians in the nation's Ivy League schools, top state universities, and research institutes. Many of the professors teach in, or occupy endowed chairs of, Africana Studies programs, and others do so in social science and humanities departments. As a part of their educational adjustment effort, however, they encouraged and sponsored their children's study of natural science subjects like physics, biology, and microbiology, or physical science and technology, including aerospace, mechanical and chemical engineering, and computer science. Also, in the past decade, more and more young Nigerian Americans have been graduating from top American medical and law schools in great numbers.

It is this second generation of Nigerian immigrants that found it easy to obtain the kinds of jobs that could make mainstream American employers assist foreign-born Nigerians in obtaining their green cards or becoming citizens through naturalization very quickly. And they are the ones whose adjustment to American socioeconomic institutions seem too easy and effortless to other Nigerians.

In addition to their services in education, Nigerian Americans have been rendering other professional services to the nation. Some of them have their own hospitals, medical clinics and laboratories, pharmacies, and nursing homes that cater to the needs of the sick and the infirm. Also, they own law firms that offer legal services to those who need assistance in the courts and in other legal matters. Furthermore, Nigerian professionals hold public offices in the states where they live or in federal establishments where they work. For example, three of the Nigerian Americans profiled in the next section hold such public offices: Dr. John O. Agwunobi, who serves as Florida state secretary of health; Dr. Emmanuel G. Mdurvwa, who is the public health officer and Bioterrorism Laboratory training and response coordinator for the state of New Hampshire; and Diogu K. Diogu, who is a senior aerospace engineering specialist at NASA–Johnson Space Center in Houston, Texas.

As the achievements and contributions of Nigerian Americans are being spotlighted in this chapter, worthy of special note are the distinguished roles that women are playing. For instance, Dr. Henrietta Ukwu, an expert in infectious diseases, serves as vice president and head of worldwide affairs of Merck Research Laboratories. She played a crucial role in the discovery of VARIVAX PLA (chicken pox vaccine) and of CRIXIVAN NDA (HIV protease inhibitor), which has alleviated the suffering of HIV/AIDS patients. And Ngozi Okonjo-Iweala is currently serving as World Bank vice president and corporate secretary in Washington, D.C.

SPORTS AND ENTERTAINMENT

In the United States, where people work hard every day, one cannot overemphasize the importance of sports and entertainment as sources of getting money, entertainment, and relaxation. Nigerian Americans are among the best in the sports world. In the 2002 season, they were members of twelve of the thirty-two professional National Football League (NFL) teams: Baltimore Ravens, Chicago Bears, Cincinnati Bengals, Detroit Lions, Indianapolis Colts, Miami Dolphins, New Orleans Saints, Philadelphia Eagles, Pittsburgh Steelers, San Diego Chargers, San Francisco 49ers, and Washington Redskins. Some of the teams had more than one Nigerian American player; and many of the players have been leading their teams to many victories. For instance, Christian Okoye played for the Kansas City Chiefs for seven years. He was so indomitable on the football field that he was called "the Nigerian Nightmare." His achievements with that team earned him a place in the Kansas City Hall of Fame, after he retired, on March 4, 2000.

Nigerian American players have also shown the same level of dedicated service in the National Basketball Association (NBA), and many of them play

Hakeem "The Dream" Olajuwon of the Houston Rockets playing against the New York Knicks in 1994. Photo by Getty Images.

for such professional teams as the Houston Rockets, L.A. Clippers, Orlando Magic, and Utah Jazz. The most famous and decorated among them is Hakeem "The Dream" Olajuwon, who led the Houston Rockets to win two consecutive NBA Championships in 1994 and 1995 (see appendix).

Nigerian American football and basketball players exhibit the same level of dedication and service on the high school and college levels, which qualifies them to be hired by college and professional teams, respectively, later in their athletic careers. What is noteworthy about their achievements is that each of them has to finish their education first before getting into professional games, and neither football nor basketball was a game they took seriously in their native Nigeria, where soccer (called *football* there) is king of all athletic games. Instead, on arriving in the United States, they kept up their interest in soccer by teaching elementary and high school students how to play the game for fun, in the 1960s and 1970s.

CULTURAL ENRICHMENT

Nigerian Americans, alongside other black Africans, have greatly influenced and modified the black culture in the United States. African Americans wear Nigerian-made clothes, especially during the Black History Month and Kwanza celebrations. The clothes are usually made of assorted cotton fabrics, such as tie-dye, brocade, printed wax, especially handwoven Akwaete cloths, and lace. Traditionally, the apparel that is made with these materials is artistically embroidered and sewn to distinguish the titles, the ethnic group, the socioeconomic class, the gender and, most recently, the political party of their wearers. There has even been some such traditional apparel made for the president of Nigeria and the first lady. These kinds of clothes are for formal occasions.

But generally, there are other kinds of Nigerian clothing made for fashion and for everyday use, which fashion dealers export to the United States or visiting Nigerian Americans bring in to family and friends. African American clergy, graduating college students, choirs, and other religious and social organizations buy and wear caps, scarves, and uniforms that are made of Nigerian fabrics at special ceremonial occasions, as a mark of honor and distinction.

Besides, many Americans of African descent purchase and proudly display in their homes and offices African artifacts, such as masks, mats, the gong and

Wedding guests in traditional clothes. Photographed by Polycarp Okeke.

the flute, and earrings and bracelets, as well as other historical icons for beauty, pride, and expression of their Africanness. During celebrative occasions, the Africana people enjoy Nigerian High life and Juju music and dance as well as being served their kind of cuisine (described in Chapter 4), all of which give everybody a fraternal feeling and psychic escape to continental Africa.

On the other hand, Nigerian Americans have embraced some of those aspects of the American culture that are peculiarly African American: their food, their music and entertainment, their hairstyles, their church services and worship, and, in some cases, their speech patterns and mannerisms. In other words, each of the two ethnic groups of black Americans has directly or indirectly modified the other's culture; in doing so, they both have brought some form of resourcefulness that has strengthened their Africanness in a society where both groups are striving to be recognized as a viable strand in the cultural tapestry of the United States.

ECONOMIC CONTRIBUTIONS

The early Nigerian immigrants contributed their labor first to American institutions of higher learning, whose graduates found employment in all sectors of the American economy. The Nigerians saved the institutions some labor costs in that those institutions hired Nigerian scholars as adjunct professors, as research/teaching assistants, or as teaching associates. Therefore, they were not paid salaries that were at par with those paid to other Americans who were in full-time, tenured positions.

Also, when Nigerians became immigrants officially, they started contributing their labor in education, agriculture, sports, entertainment, and public service. In every case, they paid their taxes and contributed services that yielded money to the local, state, and federal institutions in which they worked. We have just seen that some of them play in the NFL and NBA, the two biggest money-yielding athletic games in the United States. The money they make for their teams adds a lot to the economic resources of their host towns and cities and to the federal government coffers.

More importantly, with American attention focused on Nigeria as a reliable ally in the war against short oil supply by OPEC in the face of Middle East crisis, Nigerian Americans have been working with the Nigerian government and its diplomatic mission in the United States to ensure that American citizens do not suffer from a lot of the effects of the energy crisis that continue to threaten our economy. Furthermore, Nigerian Americans have worked hard to ensure that Nigeria remains a major trade partner of the United States in the subregion of Africa, especially in the oil sector. And Nigerians buy many manufactured goods, such as computers, Coca-Cola products, clothing, TV, shoes, books, cars, and steel from the United States, especially since after their civil war, when the British presence in Nigeria diminished tremendously.

Finally, with the adjustment they made in education and economic orientation, the Nigerian immigrants have learned to establish their own businesses: hospitals and clinics, law offices, nursing homes, grocery stores and restaurants, and fabric and beauty salons, which not only yield money to sustain the local, state, and federal economy but also employ other Americans who qualify to work in those Nigerian American businesses.

POLITICAL PARTICIPATION

Political participation is an area in which Nigerian immigrants' contributions at the moment are not very strong. However, one is not surprised by the situation, considering that many of them never knew or understood democracy in their native land, which practiced democracy only for five years and five months: from October 1960, when they attained political independence, to January 1966, when the army took over the governance of the country. But since the late 1990s, things have started to change because not only have the immigrants decided to stay permanently in the U.S, they have adjusted so well to American institutions that they have been participating politically at the local level of the American political system. The result is that, for the first time in American political history, a Nigerian American was elected the mayor of an American city in 1997. He is Rev. Emmanuel W. Onunwor, mayor of East Cleveland, Ohio. Before that he had served as the project director of the Cleveland Community Development Department, and in 1990, he became the community development director for the city of East Cleveland.

Other Nigerians are currently serving in many American city councils as advisors to the city mayors. They have begun to form political associations, including the Nigerian-American Political Action Committee, to enable them play the political game well like their fellow new immigrants.

NIGERIAN ETHNIC CHURCH

One of the social institutions that have had a strong impact on the American society is the Nigerian ethnic church. Unless one has lived in Nigeria, it is hard to fully appreciate the role of the church in the lives of Nigerians at

Emmanuel W. Onunwor, Mayor, City of East Cleveland, Ohio. Courtesy of Mayor Onunwor.

home and abroad. Virtually every educated Nigerian, except those born after the civil war, may have attended one mission school or another. That means that they took Bible Knowledge as a compulsory subject in both elementary and high school in Nigeria, and that also means that their morality was based on Christian teachings. In that society, there was no separation between state and church. Besides, they learned to "keep the Sabbath day holy," as businesses were closed and farmers did not work on their farms, even if they were non-Christians, and children were taught to "honor thy father and thy mother for length of days." But coming to the United States, where those "divine" injunctions are ostensibly not very much emphasized, family values deteriorated and divorce rates soared. Men, as heads of family, started asking why they became incapable of keeping their families together as they had done in Nigeria.

That soul-searching question led some of them to begin establishing their ethnic churches, such as the African Christian Fellowship, the Eternal Sacred Order of Cherubim and Seraphim, and the Nigerian versions of Catholic, Methodist, Anglican, Presbyterian, and Apostolic Faith denominations of the church, whose liturgical practices are different from the traditional American denominations, because the Nigerians modified theirs with their ethnic morality and worldview. Also, there are more than a hundred Catholic priests from Nigeria who are serving to make up for the shortfall in American Catholic priesthood. All those denominations of the church have since begun to counsel parents and their children on family values and respect for elders and constituted authorities; they have begun to preach acquisition of spiritual wealth above material wealth; they have begun to preach daily reading of the Bible and practical application of what they read outside the confines of the church buildings; and they have begun to emphasize holistic healing of the body, mind, and soul with medicine and prayers.

Appendix: Noted Nigerian Americans

These biographical profiles are representative of the many relatively notable Nigerian Americans whose individual achievements and contributions have benefited—and are continuing to benefit—the larger American society.

JOHN O. AGWUNOBI (1954–)
Secretary of Florida State Department of Health

Department of Health Secretary, Dr. John Agwunobi, has a wealth of experience in health care delivery, managed care, health policy and public health. Prior to becoming secretary, he diligently served the people of Florida for a year as Deputy Health Officer for Children's Medical Services. He has focused his efforts on improving access to health care and on improving the quality of certain Department of Health services. As a member of the department's leadership team, he has participated at all levels of public health planning and executive decision-making.

Dr. Agwunobi's past practice in pediatrics has included working in rural, inner city, and suburban communities. He dedicated his practice to working with underserved populations. He was born in Dundee, Scotland, and attended medical school at the University of Jos, Nigeria, where his father—a British-trained physician—was a professor of surgery. In addition to his father, Dr. Agwunobi credits his grandfather, John Shaw, for much of his passion for serving people with illness. His grandfather continued to care for his patients as a family practitioner, despite going blind, as a result of diabetes in

Dr. John Agwunobi, Secretary, Florida State Department of Health. Courtesy of
John Agwunobi.

the prime of his career. In addition to his medical degree, Dr. Agwunobi
holds an M.B.A. from Georgetown University in Washington, D.C., and is
currently seeking his Master's of Public Health from the Johns Hopkins
School of Public Health.

Dr. Agwunobi moved to Washington, D.C., in 1990, where he completed
his pediatric residency at Howard University Hospital. His training included
rotating between Children's National Medical Center and the District of
Columbia General Hospital, one of the nation's busiest inner-city hospitals.
It was there that he became interested in children with disabilities and
patients with special needs, particularly in urban communities.

In June 1993, Dr. Agwunobi joined the medical staff at the Hospital for
Sick Children, a Washington, D.C., based pediatric rehabilitation hospital
and community health care provider. He became the Medical Director in July
1998. A year later, he was named Vice President of Medical Affairs and

Patient Services. He simultaneously served as medical director for an affiliated managed care plan, where he maintained a network of more than 2,300 physicians and specialists. Understanding the myriad of challenges patients and their families face, and the importance of disease prevention, he worked to improve benefits and utilization management systems; developed new guidelines, policies, and procedures; and revitalized preventative clinical programs.

Dr. Agwunobi has a passion for leadership and innovation and sees his role as Secretary as one of team building, public service, and public health quality improvement.

(Profile reproduced by permission of John Agwunobi.)

DIOGU KALU DIOGU (1959–)
Senior Aerospace Engineering Specialist

Diogu (a.k.a. Mark) Kalu Diogu was born in the former British colony of West Cameroon to Nigerian parents, who hail from Ihechiowa in Arochukwu Local Government Area (LGA), Abia State of Nigeria. His family believed so strongly in good upbringing and education of their children that his father prophetically nicknamed him and his brother "Driver" and "Mechanic"—mechanical engineer and electrical engineer, respectively—when they were in grade school. Currently, they both are trained engineers (and his brother has a Ph.D. in electrical engineering).

Diogu is a senior aerospace engineering specialist, an expert in Earth and extraterrestrial exploration vehicle systems, and a technical manager for NASA/JSC University Research Program at NASA–Johnson Space Center in Houston, Texas. Also, he is registered to practice law in the states of Texas and New York.

His earned degrees include a B.Sc. and M.Sc. in aerospace engineering and applied mathematics from Texas A&M University System, a J.D. from Thurgood Marshal School of Law, and an L.L.M. in intellectual property law from the University of Houston Law Center.

To date, Diogu has over twenty years of experience in aeronautics and space exploration system concept, design, development, and operation. And during those years, he led other officers in the conduct and management of complex research, design, and development of programs for near Earth and extraterrestrial exploration systems, and he has also published papers on numerous topics on intellectual property law and aerospace engineering.

What he considers the greatest of his many accomplishments is leading a team of engineers that provided the shuttle with the capability for more than one landing opportunity at Kennedy Space Center (KSC). In one instance, after a failed attempt to land due to bad weather or high crosswinds at KSC, the shuttle was diverted to Andrews Air Force Base in California at a very high processing cost to NASA and the American people.

Some of his other accomplishments after graduating from college include the following:

- associate engineer in support of research and development on space transportation system (space shuttle) descent design system team;
- lead and principal engineer for guidance, navigation, and control system for space shuttle entry design and targeting and was specifically responsible for the design and development of entry targeting for STS-1 through STS-9 (first nine space shuttle flights) including the international space station logistics and operations systems;
- senior system engineering specialist responsible for design, development, operations, logistics, supportability, resource management and utilization for TransHab (TransHab is a transit habitation vehicle intended to for human habitation Earth and extraterrestrial exploration);
- senior aerospace engineering specialist responsible for reliability, risk analysis, maintainability analysis, and systems architectures with primary emphasis on development of next generation of space systems for missions beyond Earth orbit, including research and development of advanced space systems and exploration vehicles, to enable extraterrestrial construction, supportability and resource management and utilization; and
- project manager supportability and operation concept, design and development for first lunar outpost and lunar and Mars program ninety-day study to determine the feasibility of such exploration.

Diogu Kalu Diogu continues to work for NASA because of his invaluable and vast experience and leadership roles in this very important American national institution and service.

PHILIP EMEAGWALI (1954–)
Mathematician and Computer Scientist

Philip Emeagwali was born in Akure, Western Nigeria, to Igbo parents. He abandoned his high school education because of the outbreak of the Nigeria-

Philip Emeagwali, mathematician and computer scientist. Courtesy of Philip Emeagwali.

Biafra War, which drove him to Igboland, where he lived in a refugee camp. And at the end of the war, he left school a second time because his parents could not pay the fees. But after receiving some private tutoring, he took and passed the General Certificate in Education examination conducted by the University of London and was awarded a certificate, the equivalent of a high school diploma, in 1973. He then applied for and won a scholarship to study at Oregon State University. His travel from Nigeria to that institution marked the beginning of his immigration to the United States.

From 1977 to 1993, Emeagwali was engaged in graduate studies and research as well as in professional practice at Howard University (civil engineering), University of Maryland (mathematics), University of Michigan (scientific computing), University of Minnesota (supercomputing), and Army High Performance Computing Research Laboratory (research fellow).

For six years, he served as a distinguished lecturer in both the Institute of Electrical and Electronics Engineers (the world's largest technical organization) and the Association for Computing Machinery (the oldest computer society). In addition, he has delivered many major lectures all over the world, especially at the Massachusetts Institute of Technology, the United Nations

Educational, Scientific, and Cultural Organization (UNESCO), and the International Congress on Industrial and Applied Mathematics.

In 1974, Emeagwali read a 1922 science fiction article on how to use 64,000 mathematicians to forecast the weather for the whole Earth. Inspired by that article, he worked out a theoretical scheme for using 64,000 far-flung processors that could be evenly distributed around the Earth to forecast the weather. He called it a HyperBall *inter*national *net*work of computers, which became the *Internet.*

Initially his proposal to use 64,000 computers to form an international network was rejected by peers on the grounds that it would be "impossible" to achieve. Denied funding and employment for a decade, he quietly developed and published his calculations in a thousand-page monograph that described the hypothetical use of 64 binary thousand—the equivalent of 65,536—processors to perform the world's fastest computation.

In 1987, an experimental hypercube computer with 65,536 processors became available at the Los Alamos National Laboratory in New Mexico, the U.S. government's prime nuclear weapons research center. Frustrated by their inability to program 65,536 processors to simulate nuclear blasts, the Los Alamos officials had a hunch to allow physicists to simulate problems similar to theirs. Fearing that the lab officials would not accept him if it was known that he was black, Emeagwali decided to submit his proposal remotely. The lab officials approved his usage of its computers, and he remotely programmed 65,536 processors in Los Alamos while living in Michigan.

As reported by CNN, "It was his formula that used 65,000 separate computer processors to perform 3.1 billion calculations per second in 1989.... That feat led to computer scientists comprehending the capabilities of supercomputers and the practical applications of creating a system that allowed multiple computers to communicate" (CNNfyi.com, February 9, 2001; accessed December 30, 2002).

Emeagwali's discovery started making front-page headlines and cover stories in 1989, a feat that is a rarity in science. (*Time* magazine reported that the odds of a scientist "becoming even a little bit famous are a lot worse than 5,000 to 1.") And, the *Chronicle of Higher Education* (June 27, 1990) printed that "Philip Emeagwali, who took on an enormously difficult problem and, like most students working on Ph.D. dissertations, solved it alone, has won computation's top prize, captured in the past only by seasoned research teams.... If his program can squeeze out a few more percentage points, it will help decrease U.S. reliance on foreign oil."

With his success, academic journals that formerly rejected his work began singing his praises: "The amount of money at stake is staggering. For example, you can typically expect to recover 10 percent of a field's oil, if you can improve your production schedule to get just 1 million," wrote the 1989 Gordon Bell Prize Committee in the academic journal *Software* (May 1990).

In the bimonthly news journal of the Society for Industrial and Applied Mathematics, mathematician Alan Karp wrote, "I have checked with several reservoir engineers who feel that his calculation is of real importance and very fast. His explicit method not only generates lots of megaflops, but solves problems faster than implicit methods. Emeagwali is the first to have applied a pseudo-time approach in reservoir modeling" (*SIAM News,* May 1990).

His success in using 64 binary-thousand processors gave credibility and renewed interest in his formerly rejected proposal to use 64 thousand far-flung computers to forecast the weather for the whole Earth. Because the topology of his rejected international network of computers was similar to, but predated that of, the Internet, it was rediscovered and called an "idea that was ahead of its time" and a "germinal seed of the Internet." For his contributions, Emeagwali was profiled in the documentary *History of the Internet* as an Internet pioneer; he was voted one of the twenty innovators of the Internet; and CNN called him "A Father of the Internet."

A measure of his impact is that he was awarded with the 1989 Gordon Bell Prize (supercomputing's Nobel Prize) for his contributions that, in part, inspired the petroleum industry to purchase one in every ten supercomputers.

Emeagwali's improvement of computer power, or derivatives of it, is used every day by most people. His invention of how to use 65,000 processors to perform 3.1 billion calculations, in part, inspired the following:

- Apple Computer to use two processors to achieve 3.1 billion calculations per second in its Power Mac G4 computers;
- IBM to use a thousand processors to achieve 3.1 trillion calculations per second;
- IBM to plan to use 65,000 processors to manufacture the world's fastest supercomputer; and
- the reinvention of all computers to use several processors to improve their performance.

In a given week, thirty thousand students use his Web site emeagwali.com to prepare their homework assignments. Material from his Web site is frequently reprinted in small newspapers across Africa.

Another measure of his influence is that one million students have written biographical essays on him—thousands wrote to thank him for inspiring them. President Bill Clinton called him a powerful role model for young people and used the phrase "another Emeagwali" to describe children with the potential to become computer geniuses.

Emeagwali considers himself to be "a black scientist with a social responsibility to communicate science to blacks in diaspora" (CNNfyi.com, February 9, 2001; accessed December 30, 2002). In other words, he has a dual sensibility of being deeply rooted in science while using it as a tool to remind his people in the diaspora of where they have been and who they are. Dubbed a "renaissance man" by the media, he is admired not just for his enormous scientific contributions but for his deep and broad knowledge of literature and the arts. The media contacts him daily for interviews on issues as diverse as brain drain, Islamic fundamentalism, and the future of the Internet.

During his career, Emeagwali has received more than one hundred prizes, awards, and honors. These include the Computer Scientist of the Year Award of the National Technical Association (1993), Distinguished Scientist Award of the World Bank (1998), Best Scientist in Africa Award of the Pan African Broadcasting, Heritage, and Achievement Awards (2001), Gallery of Prominent Refugees of the United Nations (2001), profiled in the book *Making It in America* (Simon and Schuster, 1995) as one of the "400 models of eminent Americans," and in *Who's Who in 20th Century America* (Marquis *Who's Who*, 2000). And in a televised speech, the former president Bill Clinton described Emeagwali as "one of the great minds of the Information Age."

Emeagwali is married to Dr. Dale Emeagwali, a graduate of Georgetown University School of Medicine and winner of the 1996 Scientist of the Year Award of the National Technical Association for her cancer research. They both live near Washington, D.C., with their son, Ijeoma.

(Profile reproduced with permission of Philip Emeagwali.)

EMMANUEL G. MDURVWA (1956–)
Public Health Officer

Dr. Emmanuel G. Mdurvwa is the Bioterrorism Laboratory training and response coordinator for the state of New Hampshire. He came to the New Hampshire Public Health Laboratories from Tuskegee University in Alabama, where he served as the co-coordinator of the Research Centers for Minority Institutions (RCMI) research program. He began his professional career as Zonal Veterinary Officer in the Ministry of Forestry and Animal Resources in Maiduguri, Borno State, Nigeria. During his service there, he developed and implemented several vaccination, prophylactic, and meat inspection programs for the cattle industry, including a surveillance program for monitoring zoonotic diseases in food animals, as well as the implementation of prophylactic deworming programs. Later in 1985, he transferred his services to a newly started veterinary school at the University of Maiduguri.

Dr. Mdurvwa earned a D.V.M. degree from Ahmadu Bello University, Nigeria, in 1981, a master's degree in veterinary science at Tuskegee University in 1987, and a Ph.D. in immunology and microbiology in 1992 from Auburn University, Alabama. Later on, he received the M.P.H. degree in international health and epidemiology from the School of Public Health, University of Alabama at Birmingham, in 1999.

As an accomplished researcher and teacher, Dr. Mdurvwa has taught numerous courses at the undergraduate and graduate levels. He has also served as coinvestigator of research projects, which attracted grants in excess of $6,000,000. In addition, he has authored and coauthored thirty-five articles and abstracts for presentations at professional meetings and conferences. And his passion for community service led him to serve as a volunteer counselor for people at risk, including those living with AIDS and HIV infection in the South East region of Alabama from 1997 to 2000.

Dr. Mdurvwa is a member of several professional organizations, and he currently serves on several departmental and state committees in the state of New Hampshire, which include the biosafety, shipping, emergency response, and emergency taskforce committees. Currently, he is the chair of the emergency taskforce committee and acts as a liaison between the state laboratory and other bureaus on bioterrorism issues.

J. 'EMEKA NKWUO (1944–)
Biostatistician

Born to Igbo parents in Bukuru, Plateau State of Nigeria, Jonathan Chukwuemeka Nkwuo attended St. Peter's Anglican School, Bukuru, and Igbo National School, Aba, where he was always a top student in his classes. He scored A1 in six major subjects, which was a stellar performance at the West African School Certificate exam. He completed his Higher School studies at King's College, Lagos, where, in 1965, he obtained the best result in West Africa with A1 in pure mathematics, applied mathematics, physics, and chemistry.

Nkwuo attended the University of Ibadan and graduated with a B.Sc. Mathematics, First Class Honors, in 1972. For three consecutive years, he was awarded the faculty of science best student prize, the Adekunle Kukoyi prize in mathematics, and the Nupemco prize in science. Overall, his outstanding performance in his final year earned him the University of Ibadan Post Graduate scholarship, tenable anywhere in the world.

Deferring his postgraduate scholarship, Nkwuo worked for Shell-BP Petroleum Development Company of Nigeria. There he trained as a computer programmer, and in 1972 he became one of the first group of Nigerian trained computer programmers. He rapidly advanced in the Shell-BP organization to become in charge of the personnel-payroll system.

With the zeal to advance still burning in him, Nkwuo terminated his employment with Shell-BP in September 1973, activated his University of Ibadan Post Graduate scholarship, and headed for the graduate school at the University of California, Berkeley. There he obtained a master's degree in computer science and, in 1978, a Ph.D. in mathematical statistics.

He has held increasingly responsible positions in corporate America since 1975: From 1975 to 1978, he served as a unit supervisor at Wells Fargo Bank in San Francisco. He supervised a group responsible for the manual simulation of an automated credit scoring and collection system.

With the doctoral degree in hand, Nkwuo joined Westinghouse Data Score Systems in 1978 as a statistical analyst and was responsible for the California Assessment Program, an educational measurement system for the sixth through twelfth grades in California.

From 1980 to 1983, he was employed as a biostatistician for Syntex Laboratories, where he authored several phase III clinical trials reports for the ever popular arthritis drug NAPROXEN and the current over the counter painkiller ALEVE (Naproxen Sodium). Later in 1983, he accepted a position in New York with Ayerst Laboratories as a senior biostatistician, and hence moved from California to New York.

In 1984, after one year with Ayerst Laboratories, he quit and joined the Demand Analysis and Forecasting Research group at the telecommunications company Bell Communications Research. He became well known in the telecommunications demand analysis and forecasting community as a regular speaker in their conferences. In 1991, he was awarded the Best Presentation Award at the National Telecommunications Forecasting Conference in Boston.

In 1993, Nkwuo was inducted into the Bell Communications Research Corporate Pipeline Development Program, a training pool for all future leaders of the corporation. Since then, he has attended executive management training sessions at the Center for Creative Leadership in North Carolina, Wharton School of Business at the University of Pennsylvania, the Fuqua School of Business at Duke University, and the University of Michigan Business School.

Currently, 'Emeka Nkwuo is the lead systems engineer for the Corporate Gateway Data Engineering and Interconnection group at Telecordia Technologies, the new name for Bell Communications Research.

He is married to Emelda Ngozi Nkwuo, and they have five children.

EUCHARIA E. NNADI (1954–)
Former UMES Vice President of Academic Affairs

Eucharia E. Nnadi is the former Vice President of Academic Affairs at the University of Maryland, Eastern Shore (UMES). She came to UMES from Howard University where she served as the Dean of the College of Pharmacy and Pharmaceutical Sciences. In 1981, she began her academic career as an Assistant Professor of Pharmacy Administration at the College of Pharmacy and Pharmaceutical Sciences, Florida A&M University (FAMU) in Tallahassee, Florida. Nnadi became the first female full professor at FAMU's College of Pharmacy and Pharmaceutical Sciences in 1989, and in 1994 the first black female Dean for a U.S. College/School of Pharmacy.

Nnadi earned the B.S. degree in Pharmacy cum laude from Creighton University in Nebraska in 1977; an M.S. degree in Hospital Pharmacy in 1978; and a Ph.D. degree in Social and Administrative Pharmacy in 1982 from the University of Minnesota. She received her J.D. degree in law with high honors from the College of Law at Florida State University in 1993. Also, she has since received training in many service areas, including Dispute Resolution Using Mediation, Total Quality Management, and Leadership Training, and Fund-raising.

Also, Nnadi is an experienced and accomplished teacher, researcher and prolific writer. She has taught numerous university courses at the graduate and undergraduate levels. She served as principal or coinvestigator on grants totaling more than a million dollars. She has authored and coauthored over fifty articles/abstracts, some chapters in textbooks, a textbook, *Health Research, Design and Methodology* published by C.R.C. Press, and another textbook, *Human Resources Management for Health Care Professionals* published by Howard University Press.

Nnadi has received numerous honors and awards: She was inducted into Rho Chi Honor Society in 1976; at FAMU, she was awarded the Faculty Incentive Award for Dedication and Outstanding Service in 1985, and the Golden Pen Award for greatest number of publications in 1988; and at FSU College of Law, she received three book awards in 1991 and 1992 for earning the highest grades in select subjects. She graduated in the top 8 percent of her law class in 1993, even as she shouldered the responsibilities of a professor and mother simultaneously. Besides, Nnadi was inducted into the Order Coif Law Honor Society for her achievement in law school. She received the Pharmacist Award from the Maryland Pharmaceutical Society in May 1996, and was listed in *International Who's Who of Professionals* the same year.

Nnadi is a member of several national professional organizations in which she served and continues to serve on some of their committees, including the College Board, Middle States Region, National Association of State Universities and Land-Grant Colleges Council of Academic Affairs, the American Council on Pharmaceutical Education (ACPE) Accreditation Site Visits Team for Colleges and Schools of Pharmacy, USP, National Association of Boards Pharmacy, National Association of Boards of Pharmacy–Item Writer, and Reviewer for Texas Higher Education Coordinating Board Health Affairs Division. Eucharia E. Nnadi is also a licensed pharmacist and attorney.

(Profile reproduced with permission of Eucharia E. Nnadi.)

PETER UCHENNA NWANGWU (1949–)
Scientist, Inventor, and Entrepreneur

Peter Nwangwu was born in Umuahia, Nigeria, to Igbo parents from Anambra State. He received his high-school education from the Anglican Grammar School, Umuahia, and Methodist College, Uzuakoli, where he became the pioneer recipient of the Best Student of the Year award in 1970.

In January 1972, Nwangwu came to the United States for his college education at the University of Nebraska at Lincoln. He placed out of many courses offered by various departments and was elected into the university's honor roll beginning from his first year and later into the scholarly honor society Phi Eta Sigma. While in college, Nwangwu held several part-time jobs, including teaching assistant in biology, proctor of physics and laboratory research assistant in botany, and research assistant at the radiochemistry laboratory. The primary focus of his work in the radiochemistry lab was the use of neutron activation analysis for development of new analytical techniques for qualitative and quantitative measurement of trace elements in biological samples that employed nuclear reactors.

He earned a bachelor of science degree in chemistry from the University of Nebraska at Lincoln in May 1974, and a master's degree from the Department of Medicinal Chemistry and Pharmacognosy and the Department of Pharmacodynamics and Toxicology in 1976. His doctoral training at the

University of Nebraska Medical Center was in combined medical sciences, with special focus on Pharmacology. He made history when he became the first student at that university to earn the Pharm.D. and Ph.D. degrees simultaneously. Nwangwu's dissertation, titled "The Antirrhythmic Activities, Acute Toxicity Profile, and Hemodynamic Properties of some New and Selected Quinidine Analogs," involved the development and pharmacological characterization of seven new quinidine analogs (antiarrhythmic drugs), which are protected by U.S. patents.

In addition to the development of the seven new drugs, Nwangwu's career as an inventor includes the invention of two new research techniques in pharmacology that received worldwide acceptance when they were published in scientific literature. His in vivo technique for screening antiarrhythmic agents in mice has been used by many scientists in various parts of the world because the method is economical and allows the use of large numbers of small animals, which is significant for statistical purposes. He also invented and published about a new technique for the identification of time of myocardial infarction employing TC-99 pyrophosphate.

In 1979, Nwangwu accepted a professional position as director of clinical research and assistant professor of pharmacology and toxicology at Florida A&M University in Tallahassee, Florida. In 1981, he became Associate Professor of Pharmacology and Toxicology at St. John's University, New York.

Concerned over the years about the lack of accessibility to quality health care for many poor people, especially in the developing countries of the world, Nwangwu founded a generic drug manufacturing company in Houston, Texas, whose operational profits are devoted to humanitarian causes, in the form of improving the quality and accessibility of health care for the poor. Consequently, he left Ayerst Laboratories to become president of Punlabs Quality Products, Ltd., and Ebony Pharmaceutical Manufacturing, Inc.

Currently, Nwangwu holds the following positions: president and chairman of the board, Universal Pharmacy Consultants, Inc; president and chairman of the board, the Infinity Group, Inc; president and chairman of the board, South Atlantic Petroleum, Inc.; chairman, board of directors, Presidential Hotels Development Group, Inc.; and chairman, board of directors, St. Pierre du Paris, Inc.; all in Dallas, Texas.

Nwangwu has received many awards and honors, including being listed in more than twenty biographical reference books. Also, he has published more than forty articles in major medical and scientific journals. His book *Concepts and Strategies in New Drug Development* (Praeger, 1983) is widely used in pharmaceutical industries and clinical pharmacology training programs throughout the United States, Canada, and Europe. He has served on the edi-

torial/advisory boards of national and international scientific/medical journals, including *Methods and Findings in Experimental and Clinical Pharmacology; Drugs of Today; Drugs of the Future;* and *Clinical Toxicology Consultant.*
He is Fellow of the American College of Clinical Pharmacology and Fellow of
the American Society of Consultant Pharmacists.

Peter Nwangwu is married to Patience Nwangwu, and they have five sons
and one daughter.

E. OKECHUKWU ODITA (1936–)
Artist and Art Historian

E. Okechukwu Odita was born in Nigeria and came to the United States
in 1964 for graduate studies in fine arts. He earned his Diploma in Fine Arts
in Painting from the Nigeria College of Arts, Science and Technology, Zaria,
Nigeria (1962); a Master's of Arts in Printmaking from the University of Iowa
(January 1965); a Master's of Fine Arts in Painting from the University of
Iowa (August 1965); and a Ph.D. in History of African Art from Indiana
University (1970).

Odita has held several academic positions at such schools as the University
of Nigeria, Nsukka; Indiana University; The Ohio State University, Columbus; and Alvan Ikoku College of Education, Owerri, Nigeria.

He began teaching History of Traditional African Art in 1969 and Contemporary African Art in 1978, both at The Ohio State University. And he is
the creator of the first graduate program in History of Contemporary African
Art in the United States. The courses he offers on the undergraduate and
graduate levels in the history of African art span two fields of study: African
Art and Archaeology and Contemporary African Art. In addition to teaching
those courses, he has published extensively in the field.

As an artist and art historian, Odita has conducted over twenty national
and international exhibitions. The honors and awards that E. Okechukwu
Odita has garnered include three Silver Medals and five First Class certifi-
cates from the Eastern Nigeria Festival of Arts (1955); Nigerian Federal
Scholarship Awards (1959–60); U.S. Agency for International Development
(USAID) Scholar Awards (1963–65); Aggrey Fellow, International Phelps-
Stokes Fund (1966–68); and the Pan-African Research Award, USA (1975).

By way of rewarding the two countries that have nurtured his academic
and professional development and practice, Odita started in summer 2001
the program International K–12 Art Teachers Workshop Nigeria, which is
held annually in Nigeria. It is a linkage program between The Ohio State

Artist E. Okechukwu Odita at work. Courtesy of E. Okechukwu Odita.

University, where he currently works, and the Federal Republic of Nigeria, his native country, where he conducts workshops on Philosophy of African Art, Contemporary African Art, and Cyber Link Center. Odita's team includes American professors and graduate students and their Nigerian counterparts, who take African art education to the people in Nigerian major cities and rural communities.

E. Odita is married to Florence Odita, the former bureau chief, Office of Research and Program Evaluation, Ohio State Department of Human Services, and currently is a trial lawyer in Columbus, Ohio. They have four children.

KEMNAGUM KEN OKORIE (1950–)
Trial Lawyer and Former Secretary-General, World Igbo Congress

Kemnagum Ken Okorie, born in Nigeria, was completing his high-school education when that country's first military coup, which took place in 1966, set in motion a chain of events that truncated democratic governance, culminating in the Nigeria-Biafra War.

In 1973, Okorie came to the United States to realize his dream of acquiring higher education that he had almost lost as a result of the brutal war. In 1977, he graduated from the University of South Florida in Tampa, with a dual degree in accounting and economics, and went on to work as an internal auditor for GTE. He earned his M.B.A. degree two years later and joined the management team of the Harte-Hanks Communications. He rapidly rose to the position of director of finance and accounting, in charge of cable-television operations.

Okorie's lifelong passion for law practice remained undiminished; he had spent a good deal of his high school vacations in Nigeria observing proceedings in courts and tribunals. In 1983, he gave up corporate life to study law at the University of Denver College of Law. While attending law school, Okorie worked for the cable-television division of Time/Life Group as senior financial analyst, where he was responsible for overseas investments. He earned a Jurist Doctor in 1986, and quickly went to Houston, where he built his law firm, Okorie and Associates, PC.

An accomplished trial lawyer, Okorie made national headlines when he successfully pioneered challenges against a little known Texas law that vested in doctors and hospitals the power to terminate care for patients on life-support without their families' input, as well as disregarding such patients' wishes. He also started a legal resistance movement that sounded the initial alarm in Texas on the excesses of homeowners' associations and their collaboration with unscrupulous management companies to exploit homeowners. A highly principled man, Okorie decided in 1995 against accepting further court appointments to defend indigents because of new restrictions he believed diminished and compromised defense lawyers' roles and put them in the position of becoming part of the court system's conspiracy to convict clients, who are merely accused but not necessarily guilty of the crime for which they were accused.

Out of his personal experiences of injustice and sufferings of his Igbo people, which emanated from the pogrom and the genocidal war that Nigeria waged against them, Okorie developed an extraordinary sense of social commitment that enabled him to organize his people for their group survival. Consequently, he devoted a significant part of his life and career to developing a variety of volunteer programs that serve people and their communities here in the United States and in his native Nigeria.

It was the same spirit of commitment that motivated him earlier, upon arriving in Houston in 1982, to promptly embrace a movement that was forming to organize Nigerians for survival in the local environment, which was hostile and notorious for selective law enforcement against them. This led to the founding of the Nigerian Foundation, whose sole purpose was to defend their individual and collective rights and interests against police brutality and other civil rights violations. Okorie was elected the first general secretary of that organization, and he served on its board for nearly ten years.

He realized early in his law practice that being unfamiliar with the justice system rendered new immigrants vulnerable and caused many of them to suffer serious and undue disadvantages. Because of that, he organized in 1990 the African Bar Association of America (ABAA) for the purpose of creating a forum for young immigrant lawyers to exchange ideas and share common problems. He served as ABAA president for seven years, during which period he also introduced a platform for a legal series, Community Legal Forum, that regularly brought together judges, lawyers, and other experienced persons to debate and explain such matters as immigration, tenant rights, family law, and other legal issues for the benefit and interest of the larger community of African immigrants.

In October 1993, when the military president of Nigeria, General Abacha, called for a constitutional conference following his seizure of power through another coup, many Nigerians in diaspora did not trust his motive. Instead, they questioned the need for a new constitution when the previous constitutions introduced in 1979 and 1989, respectively, were never implemented. But Okorie had a different idea: to organize a collective voice of Nigerians in diaspora that would impact events in their home country. He began a worldwide quest to reach out to Igbo people and organizations all over North America and Europe on the issues that troubled Nigerians everywhere. This led to the formation of the World Igbo Congress (WIC) in August 1994 as a Pan-Igbo organization whose influence on Igbo and Nigerian affairs is growing. Okorie served as its first secretary-general from 1994 to 1999.

WIC soon became a model for other ethnic Nigerian organizations worldwide, which had previously depended on informal personal contacts as the only means of starting their sociocultural organizations at various levels. That initiative Okorie took has since introduced an American orientation into Nigeria's democratization practices in a very significant way.

In 1988, the mayor and city council of Houston appointed Okorie to the Building Standards Commission, in which he is currently serving a third term as vice chairperson. A longtime YMCA volunteer, Okorie has also served on the boards of Citizens for Better Health, Job Plus, Inc., and other charitable organizations.

Kemnagum Ken Okorie is married to Lynda Ifeoma Okorie, and they have four young sons.

HAKEEM "THE DREAM" OLAJUWON (1965–)
NBA's Houston Rockets Star; President, the Dream Foundation

There is no more true tale of the American "Dream" than the story of Hakeem Olajuwon—All-Star center for the NBA's Houston Rockets.

Olajuwon (Nigerian for "always being on top") first displayed his athleticism in soccer and handball as a youth in Lagos, Nigeria. After discovering basketball at age seventeen, Hakeem left his native Nigeria in 1980, with less than one year of organized basketball experience, for the University of Houston, a college basketball powerhouse. Nicknamed "The Dream" because of his whimsical entrance into basketball and his untapped potential, Hakeem became a dominant force in college basketball with the Houston Cougars.

Olajuwon led the Cougars, known as "Phi Slamma Jamma—the world's tallest fraternity!" to three consecutive Final Four appearances (1982–84). In 1983, Hakeem was named the NCAA Tournament's Most Outstanding Player, the first player from a nonwinning team to earn such an honor in seventeen years. Olajuwon, a consensus All-American during his final season with "Phi Slamma Jamma," led the nation in rebounds, field goal percentage, and blocked shots. As a testament to his dominance, Hakeem was named the Southwest Conference "Player of the Decade" (1980s) by the media and coaches. Hakeem's impressive college career was an indication of the standards he would set in the National Basketball Association.

As the first selection in the 1984 NBA Draft, Hakeem transformed the Houston Rockets' worst-ever team (14–68 in 1982–83) into Western Conference Champions and an NBA Finalist in just his second season. Well known for his tenacious defense, relentless rebounding, and smooth offensive moves, "The Dream" is consistently among the league leaders in scoring, rebounding, blocked shots, and steals. In 1992, Hakeem was the NBA's Defensive Player of the Year, the Most Valuable Player Runner-Up, All-NBA, and *Basketball Weekly's* NBA Player of the Year.

In the preceding season, Hakeem and the Rockets reached the pinnacle of success. Hakeem led the Rockets to an NBA record tying fifteen consecutive victories to start the 1993–94 season, a franchise record of 58 wins and their first NBA Championship defeating the New York Knickerbockers in a seven-game series. Hakeem's "Dream Season" resulted in his being named the NBA's

Most Valuable Player, the NBA's Defensive Player of the Year (for the second consecutive year), and the NBA Finals' Most Valuable Player. Hakeem is the only player in the NBA's history to accomplish this remarkable achievement.

In 1995, Hakeem and the Houston Rockets relived the dream by entering the play-offs as only the sixth seed, defeating the top three teams in the NBA (Utah Jazz, Phoenix Suns, and San Antonio Spurs) in a dramatic fashion, and going to the NBA finals for the second time to win the title against the Orlando Magic.

Hakeem received the biggest honor of his illustrious career by becoming an American citizen in 1993. Since then, the way was cleared by FIBA, the international governing body of basketball, for Hakeem to play in the 1996 Olympic Games in Atlanta, Georgia. As the NBA's first foreign born MVP, Hakeem realized the international scope of the game. In fact, in the preceding season he was also selected as the International Ambassador for the NBA. Hakeem has always wanted to perform at the highest level of international competition and he looked forward to playing in the Olympics and wearing the USA Basketball uniform with honor.

Unlike most American sports celebrities, Hakeem accepts his status graciously and puts his basketball exploits in perspective. Throughout the NBA, Hakeem is known as a fearless competitor on the court, but humble, friendly, and polite off the hardwood. Hakeem dutifully accepts being a role model and is very mindful of giving back to society. He donates his time to the National Stroke Association, the American Cancer Society, and the Make-a-Wish Foundation.

In 1994, Hakeem created the "Dream Foundation" to encourage education as a way of realizing one's dreams. The foundation provides college scholarship funds for Houston-area students.

OSONYE TESS ONWUEME (1955–)
Playwright

Born in Nigeria, Osonye Tess Onwueme is one of the leading African-born playwrights and a professor of English. She was educated in two Nigerian universities: the University of Ife, Ile-Ife, where she earned her B.A. and M.A. degrees in English, and the University of Benin, where she earned a Ph.D. in literature.

Prior to coming to the United States in 1989, Onwueme taught English in two Nigerian universities—Federal University of Technology, Owerri, and the Imo State University, Okigwe—and was in charge of the performing arts in both institutions. She also served as the acting president, Association of Nigerian Authors (ANA) in 1988–89, and vice president of the same organization in 1987–88.

In the United States, Onwueme has held some professional appointments, which include distinguished writer and associate professor of African Studies, Wayne State University, Detroit, Michigan (1989–90), associate professor of English and Multicultural Literary Studies, Montclair State University, Montclair, New Jersey (1990–92), visiting professor of English and Africana Studies, Vassar College, Poughkeepsie, New York (1992–93), and distinguished professor of cultural diversity and professor of English, University of Wisconsin, Eau Claire, Wisconsin (1994–present).

As a playwright, Onwueme has published *A Hen Too Soon* (1983), *The Broken Calabash* (1984), *The Desert Encroaches* (1986), *A Scent of Onions* (1986), *Ban Empty Barn and Other Plays* (1986), *Mirror Campus* (1987), *The Reign of Wazobia and Other Plays* (1988), *Legacies* (1989), *Parable for a Season* (1991), *Riot in Heaven* (1996), *The Missing Face* (1997), *Tell It to Women* (2000), *Shakara, Dance-hall Queen* (2002), and *Then She Said It* (2002). Also, she has published a novel, *Why the Elephant Has No Butt* (2000), and a few poems and short stories.

Because of her published works and professional services, Onwueme has been given many honors and awards, which include the Martin Luther King, Jr., Caesar Chavez, and Rosa Parks Distinguished Writers Award at Wayne State University, 1990; Award for Excellence for Academic Contributions by Women of Color to the University of Wisconsin, 1995; Drama Prize of the Association of Nigerian Authors for her epic drama *Tell It to Women,* 1995; and a Drama Prize of the Association of Nigerian Authors for her play *Shakara, Dance-hall Queen.*

Osonye Tess Onwueme is an avid promoter of cultural diversity and equality for women both in her native Nigeria and here in the United States. In her works, she has been promoting female issues, especially as they affect women of color in Africa, the United States, and the Caribbean.

HILARY CHIEDU ONYIUKE (1959–)
Neurosurgeon

Dr. Hilary Chiedu Onyiuke, neurosurgeon, was born in Onitsha, South East Nigeria, to a wealthy and noble family. Upon completing his high school education at St. Gregory's College in Lagos, he entered the College of Medicine of the University of Ibadan, Nigeria, in 1977 and graduated in 1982. During his years in the medical school, he earned some distinction in human anatomy and won the E. Latunde Odeku First Prize in Neurosurgery. After his internship at Park Lane General Hospital at Enugu, he became a Nigerian Registered Medical Practitioner and was admitted into the residency program in surgery in the Department of Surgery of the College of Medicine at the University Teaching Hospital, Ibadan.

In 1985, while still a resident at Ibadan, Dr. Onyiuke successfully passed qualifying examinations to become primary fellow of Nigerian College of Surgeons, primary fellow of West African College of Surgeons, and primary fellow of the Royal College of Surgeons of England. In January 1988, he traveled to Canada, where he was admitted to full residency program in neurosurgery in the Department of Surgery at the University of Toronto. In 1990, he passed the examination of the American College of Neurological Surgeons and of the Principles of Surgery of the Royal College of Physicians and Surgeons of Canada. On completion of his residency program, he became a fellow of the Royal College of Surgeons, specializing in neurosurgery. From January 1993 to December 1993, he enrolled in a fellowship program in neurotrauma in the Division of Neurosurgery at the Sunnybrook Health Science Center (Head Trauma and Spinal Cord Injury). In 1990, Dr. Onyiuke received certification in Lougheed's Microsurgical course, University of Toronto.

He was appointed assistant professor of surgery, Division of Neurosurgery, at the University of Connecticut's School of Medicine, and neurological surgeon at the Hartford Hospital, John Dempsey Hospital, and the University of Connecticut Health Center. He was promoted to associate professor in the year 2000. Thereafter, he became director of the Head Injury Program at the Hartford Hospital, where he also served as coordinator of the Neurotrauma Fellowship Program from 1994 to 1997. In September 2000, he was appointed chairman of the Connecticut Spinal Cord Injury Research Board. He became chief of the Division of Neurosurgery at the University of Connecticut Health Center in 1999.

Dr. Onyiuke's publications include many articles and abstracts in refereed neurosurgical journals. In addition, he has served as a guest speaker to national and international medical associations, including the Affiliated Hospital of Shandong's Medical University, People's Republic of China, where he lectured on spinal cord injuries.

Dr. Onyiuke's clinical research interests reside in the field of traumatic brain injury, which involves carrying out neuroclinical trials. As a renowned neurosurgeon, he continues to make invaluable contributions in the fields of neurology and neurosurgery.

Bibliography

Achebe, Chinua. 1958. *Things Fall Apart.* London: Heinemann Educational Books, Ltd.

———. 1966. *A Man of the People.* London: Heinemann Educational Books, Ltd.

———. 1971. *Beware, Soul Brother, and Other Poems.* Enugu, Nigeria: Nwamife-lfejika.

———. 1972. *Girls at War and Other Stories.* London: Heinemann Educational Book, Ltd.

———. 1976. *Morning Yet on Creation Day.* New York: Anchor Press/Doubleday.

———. 1983. *The Trouble with Nigeria.* Enugu, Nigeria: Fourth Dimension Publishing Co., Ltd.

———. 1988. *The University and the Leadership Factor in Nigerian Politics.* Enugu, Nigeria: Abic Press.

———. 1987. *Anthills of the Savannah.* London: Heinemann Educational Books, Ltd.

———. 1988. *Hopes and Impediments: Selected Essays, 1965–87.* London: Heinemann Educational Books, Ltd.

———. 2000. *Home and Exile.* New York: Oxford University Press.

Afigbo, Adiele. 1981. *Ropes of Sand: Studies in Igbo History and Culture.* Ibadan, Nigeria: University Press, Ltd.

Amadiume, Ifi. 1987. *Male Daughters, Female Husbands: Gender and Sex in an African Society.* London: Zed Books.

Andah, Bassey W. 1991. *Nigeria's Indigenous Technology.* Ibadan, Nigeria: Ibadan University Press.

Arasanyin, Olaoba. 1997. "Learning from India's Experience: The Quest for Unilangue in Nigeria." *Journal of the Third World Spectrum* 4 (spring): 37–69.

————. 1998/99. "Surplus Agenda, Deficit Culture: Language and the Class-Divide in Nigeria." *Journal of West African Languages* 22 (October): 81–101.

Arinze, Francis A. 1978. *Sacrifice in Ibo Religion.* Ibadan, Nigeria: Ibadan University Press.

Ayandele, E. A., et al., eds. *The Making of Modern Africa: The Late Nineteenth Century to the Present Day.* Vol. 2. London: Longman.

Azikiwe, Nnamdi. 1961. *Zik: A Selection from the Speeches of Nnamdi Azikiwe.* London: Cambridge University Press.

————. 1970. *My Odyssey: An Autobiography.* London: C. Hurst.

Barth, Frederick, ed. 1998. *Ethnic Groups and Boundaries: The Social Organization of Culture Difference.* Prospect Heights, IL: Waveland Press.

Basden, G. T. 1966. *Among the Ibos of Nigeria.* London: Frank Cass.

Beazley, C. Raymond. 1967. *Prince Henry the Navigator.* New York: Barnes and Noble.

Bell-Gam, Ruby A., and David Uru Iyam, compilers. 1985. *Nigeria.* Vol. 100, *World Bibliographical Series.* Santa Barbara, CA: Clio Press.

Bennet Jr., Lerone. 1981. *Before the Mayflower: A History of Black America.* Harmondsworth, U.K.: Penguin.

Benson, Dayo, and Wale Akinlola. 2001. "Obasanjo's Opponents Back Rimi." http://www.ngrguardiannews.com/news2/nn850218.html, accessed March 2, 2002.

Blalock Jr., Hubert M. 1967. *Toward a Theory of Minority-Group Relations.* New York: John Wiley.

Brown, Lawrence Guy. 1969. *Immigration: Cultural Conflicts and Social Adjustments.* New York: Longmans, Green and Co.

Canot, Theodore, 1928. *Adventures of an African Slaver.* New York: Garden City Publishing Co.

Cary, Joyce. 1962. *The Case for African Freedom and Other Writings on Africa.* Austin: University of Texas Press.

Chinweizu, Chinweizu. 1975. *The West and the Rest of Us.* New York: Random House.

————. 1987. *Decolonizing the African Mind.* Lagos, Nigeria: Pero Publishing Co.

————. 1994. *Recolonizing or Reparation.* Lagos, Nigeria: International Committee for Reparation.

Collin, Robert C., ed. 1969. *The Partition of Africa: Illusion or Necessity?* New York: John Wiley.

Conrad, Joseph. 1983. *Heart of Darkness.* Edited by Paul O'Prey. London: Penguin.

Crowder, Michael. 1978. *The Story of Nigeria.* London: Faber and Faber.

"Dr. Nnamdi Azikiwe, 16 November 1904–11 May 1996, 'Zik of Africa': The Early Years, Part One." http://www.greatepicbooks.com/epics/november98.html, accessed December 10, 2001.

Ekwe-Ekwe, Herbert. 1990a. *The Biafran War: Nigeria and the Aftermath.* Lewiston, NY: Edwin Mellen Press.

———. 1990b. *Conflict and Intervention in Africa: Nigeria, Angola, Zaire.* New York: St. Martin's.

Emeagwali, Philip. 2002. "It Was the Audacity of My Thinking: History of the Internet." http://emeagwali.com/history/internet/index/html, accessed July 20, 2002.

Emenyonu, Ernest N. 1971. "African Literature: What Does It Take to Be Its Critic?" *African Literature Today* 5: 1–11.

Enekwe, Ossie. 1987. *Igbo Masks: The Oneness of Ritual and Theater.* Lagos, Nigeria: Nigeria Magazine.

Equiano, Olaudah. 1814. *The Interesting Narrative of the Life of Olaudah Equiano, or Gustavus Vassa, the African, Written by Himself.* Leeds, UK: James Nichols.

Ezickson Jr., Aaron, ed. 1965. *The Peace Corps: A Pictorial History.* New York: Hill and Wang.

Fanon, Frantz. 1963. *The Wretched of the Earth.* Trans. Constance Farrington. London: Macgibbon and McKee.

———. 1965. *A Dying Colonialism.* Trans. Haakon Chevalier. New York: Grove.

———. 1968. *Towards the African Revolution: Political Essays.* Trans. Haakon Chevalier. New York: Grove.

———. 1969. *Black Skin, White Masks.* Trans. Charles L. Markmann. New York: Grove.

Forest, Tom. 1994. *The Growth of Nigerian Private Enterprise.* Charlottesville: University Press of Virginia.

Frazer, Sir James George. 1963. *The Golden Bough: A Study in Magic and Religion.* New York: Macmillan.

Geary, William Nevill M. 1927. *Nigeria under British Rule.* London: Methuen.

Goody, Jack. 1977. *The Domestication of the Savage Mind.* Cambridge, U.K.: Cambridge University Press.

Gourlander, Harold. 1973. *Tales of Yoruba Gods and Heroes.* Greenwich, CT: Fawcett.

Green, M. M. 1964. *Ibo Village Affairs.* Loudon: Frank Cass.

Guyer, Jane I. 1992. "Representation without Taxation: An Essay on Democracy in Rural Nigeria, 1952–1990." *African Studies Review* 35 (April): 41–79.

Hair, P. E. H., ed. 1967. *The Early Study of Nigerian Languages: Essays and Bibliographies.* Cambridge, U.K.: Cambridge University Press.

Hastings, A. C. 1925. *Nigerian Days.* London: Bodley Head.

Herberg, Will. 1955. *Protestant, Catholic, Jew.* New York: Doubleday.

Hill, Robert. 1972. *The Strength of Black Families.* New York: Emerson-Hall.

Hitchcock, Peter. 1993. *Dialogics of the Oppressed.* Minneapolis: University of Minnesota Press.

Holloway, Joseph, ed. 1991. *Africanisms in American Culture.* Bloomington: Indiana University Press.

Hurh, Won Moo. 1998. *The Korean Americans.* Westport, CT: Greenwood Press.

Hutchinson, E. P. 1981. *Legislative History of American Immigration Policy 1798–1965.* Philadelphia, PA: University of Pennsylvania Press.

Idowu, E. Bolaji. 1994. *Oladumare: God in Yaruba Belief.* New York: Wazobia Press.

Ikime, Obaro, ed. 1980. *Groundwork of Nigerian History.* Ibadan, Nigerian: Historical Society of Nigeria/Heinemann Educational Books, Ltd.

Ilesanmi, Simeon O. 1997. *Religious Pluralism and the Nigerian State.* Athens: Ohio University Press.

Isichei, Elizabeth. 1973. *The Ibo People and the Europeans: The Genesis of a Relationship—to 1906.* New York: St. Martin's.

———. 1976. *A History of the Igbo People.* London: Macmillan.

Jahn, Hanheinz, 1961. *The New African Culture.* New York: Grove.

Jefferson, Thomas. 1998. "Declaration of Independence." In *Rereading America: Cultural Contexts for Critical Thinking and Writing,* 4th ed., edited by Gary Colombo, Robert Cullen, and Bonnie Lisle, 684–87. Boston, MA: Bedford/St. Martin's.

Jemie, Onwuchekwe. 1970. *Biafran Requiem.* Port Moresby, Papua, New Guinea: Pocket Poets.

Jones, Maldwyn Allen. 1969. *American Immigration.* Chicago: University of Chicago Press.

Kennedy, John F. 1964. *A Nation of Immigrants.* New York: Harper and Row.

Kim, Young Yun. 1989. "Intercultural Adaptation." In *Handbook of International and Intercultural Communication,* edited by Molefi Kete Asante and William B. Gudykunst, 275–94. Newbury Park, CA: Sage.

King Jr., Martin Luther. 1997. "I Have a Dream." In *The Norton Anthology of African American Literature,* edited by Henry Louis Gates Jr. and Nellie Y. McKay, 80–83. New York: Norton.

Larsen, Golden. 1965. *The Dark Descent: Social Change and Moral Responsibility in the Novels of Joyce Cary.* London: Michael Joseph.

Lawrence, P. 1988. "The Political Economy of the 'Green Revolution' in Africa." *Review of African Political Economy* 42: 59–75.

Lindfors, Bernth. 1999. *The Blind Men and the Elephant and Other Essays in Biographical Criticism.* Trenton, NJ: Africa World Press.

Lugard, Sir F. D. 1922. *The Dual Mandate in British Tropical Africa.* London: Blackwood and Sons.

Mackenzie, W. J. M. 1975. *Power, Violence, Decision.* Hammondsworth, U.K.: Penguin.

Madsen, Axel. 1984. *60 Minutes: The Power and The Politics of America's Most Popular TV News Show.* New York: Dodd, Mead and Co.

Malcolm X. 1998. "Learning to Read." *Rereading America: Cultural Contexts for Critical Thinking and Writing,* 4th ed., edited by Gary Colombo, Robert Cullen, and Bonnie Lisle, 219–27. Boston, MA: Bedford/St. Martin's.

Mazrui, Ali. 1998. "Capitalism, Democracy, and Stability in Africa." http://www.usafricaonline.com/inside_a/democracy.html, accessed July 20, 2001.

Mbadiwe, K. O. 1991. *Rebirth of a Nation.* Enugu, Nigeria: Fourth Dimension.

Mbiti, John S. 1969. *African Religions and Philosophy.* New York: Frederick A. Praeger.

Meek, C. K. 1937. *Law and Authority in a Nigerian Tribe: A Study in Indirect Rule.* London: Oxford University Press.

Montagu, Ashley, ed. 1964. *The Concept of Race.* New York: Free Press of Glencoe.

Nigerian Government Printer. 1982. *First National Seminar on Agricultural Development Projects.* Kaduna, Nigeria: Federal Department of Rural Development.

Nigerian Tourism Development Corporation. 2001. *Nigeria: Beauty in Diversity.* Abuja, Nigeria: Federal Ministry of Culture and Tourism.

Njaka, Mazi Elechukwu Nnadibuagha. 1974. *Igbo Political Culture.* Evanston, IL: Northwestern University Press.

Nwachukwu, Ike. 1991. *Nigeria and the ECOWAS Since 1945.* Enugu, Nigeria: Fourth Dimension.

Nwangwu, Chido. 1996. "Azikiwe: Statesman and Titan of African Politics." http.www.hartford-hoop.com/archives/34a/008.html, accessed July 20, 2002.

———. 1998. "Walter Carrington: An African-American Puts Principle above Self for Nigeria." http:www.usafricanline.com/carrington.html, accessed July 20, 2002.

———. 1999a. "At 39, Nigerians Still Face Dishonest Stereotypes Such as Buckley's and Other Self-inflicted Wounds." http://usafricanline.com/chidonigeria39.html, accessed July 20, 2002.

———. 1999b. "Beyond U.S. Electoral Shenanigans, Rewards, and Dynamics of a Democratic Republic Holds Lessons for African Politics." http://ink2.com/nwa-ngwu11192000.htm, accessed November 11, 2000.

———. 2000. "Why Colin Powell Brings Gravitas, Credibility, and Star Power to Bush Presidency." http://www.usafricanonline.com/chidopowell.html, accessed December 11, 2001.

———. 2001. "What's Africa Have to Do with the Events of September 11 [2000]?" http://www.hartford-hwp.com/archives/349/008.html, accessed December 11, 2001.

———. 2002. "Establishing of Harvard African Law Association Is an Excellent Networking Move." http://www.usafricaonline.com/chido.halaharvard.html, accessed May 24, 2003.

Nwoga, Donatus I. 1984. *The Supreme God as Stranger in Igbo Religious Thought.* Ekwereazu, Nigeria: Hawk Press.

Obiechina, Emmanuel N. 1980. *Africa Shall Survive.* Enugu, Nigeria: Fourth Dimension.

———. 1985. *Mammon-Worship in Twentieth Century Nigeria.* Enugu, Nigeria; Afa Press.

Odumegwu-Ojukwu, Emeka. 1969. *Biafra: Random Thoughts of C. Odumegwu-Ojukwu, General of the People's Army.* New York: Harper and Row.

———. 1989. *Because I Am Involved.* Ibadan, Nigeria: Spectrum Books, Ltd.

Ogbaa, Kalu. 1981. "An Interview with Chinua Achebe." *Research in African Literatures* 12 (spring): 1–13.

———. 1994. *The Gong and the Flute: African Literary Development and Celebration.* Westport, CT: Greenwood Press.

———. 1995. *Igbo.* New York: The Rosen Publishing Group.

———. 1999. *Understanding* Things Fall Apart: *A Student Casebook to Issues, Sources, and Historical Documents.* Westport, CT: Greenwood Press.

Ojike, Mbonu. 1945. *Portrait of a Boy in Africa.* New York: East and West Association Press.

———. 1947. *I Have Two Countries.* New York: John Day.

Okeke, J. O. S. 1998. "W. I. C. on Gowon's Apology to Igbos." http://www.usafricaonline.com/inside_a/apology2igbos.html, accessed June 20, 2002.

Okorie, Kemnagum Ken. 1998. "Sierra Leone, Nigeria and Regional Politics." http://www.usafricaonline.com/inside_a/n8rp.html, accessed June 20, 2002.

Omer-Cooper, J. D., et al., eds. 1968. *The Making of Modern Africa: The Nineteenth Century to the Partition.* Vol. 1. London: Longman.

Onuora, Madu, and Victor-Onyeka Ben. 2002. "Tamuno, Haruna, Others Renew Call for National Confab." http://www.ngrguardianews.com/news2/nn850218.html, accessed July 13, 2002.

Parrillo, Vincent N. 1998. "Causes of Prejudice." In *Rereading America: Cultural Contexts for Critical Thinking and Writing,* 4th ed., edited by Gary Colombo, Robert Cullen, and Bonnie Lisle, 562–73. Boston, MA: Bedford/St. Martin's.

Phillips, Anne. 1989. *The Enigma of Colonialism: British Policy in West Africa.* Bloomington: Indiana University Press.

Reimers, D. M. 1985. *Still the Golden Door.* New York: Columbia University Press.

Rice, Gerard T. 1965. *The Bold Experiment: J.F.K.'s Peace Corps.* Notre Dame, IN: University of Notre Dame Press.

Schraeder, Peter, ed. 1992. *Intervention into the 1990s: U.S. Foreign Policy in the Third World,* 2nd ed. Boulder, CO: Lynne Reinner Publications.

Schudson, Michael. 1995. *The Power of News.* Cambridge, MA: Harvard University Press.

Sesay, Amadu, ed. 1986. *Africa and Europe: From Partition to Independence or Dependency?* Dover, NH: Croom Helm.

Shaw, Thurstan. 1980. "Prehistory." In *Groundwork of Nigerian History,* edited by Obaro Ikime, 25–53. Ibadan, Nigeria: Historical Society of Nigeria/Heinemann Educational Books, Ltd.

Shepard, Robert B. 1991. *Nigeria, America, and the United States: From Kennedy to Reagan.* Bloomington: Indiana University Press.

Simon, Rita J. 1985. *Public Opinion and the Immigrant: Print Media Coverage, 1880–1980.* Lexington, MA: D. C. Health.

Simpson, George E., and Milton J. Yinger. 1972. *Racial and Cultural Minorities.* New York: Harper and Row.

Skinner, Elliot P. 1992. *Africans and U.S. Policy Towards Africa 1850–1924: In Defense of Black Nationality.* Washington, D.C.: Howard University Press.

Solarin, Ibiyinka. 1998. "Nigeria's Challenge of the 21st Century Will Be in the Hands of Present Generation." http://www.usafricaonline.com/inside_a/ challenge.html, accessed July 13, 2002.

Soyinka, Wole. 1996. *The Open Sore of a Continent: A Personal Narrative of the Nigerian Crisis.* New York: Oxford University Press.

———. 1971. *Before the Blackout.* Ibadan, Nigeria: Orisun Acting Editions.

———. 1972. *The Man Died.* New York: Harper and Row.

———. 1988. *The Jero Plays.* London: Methuen.

———. 1999. *The Burden of Memory, the Muse of Forgiveness.* New York: Oxford University Press.

Steele, Shelby. 1998. "I'm Black, You're White, Who's Innocent?" In *Rereading America: Cultural Contexts for Critical Thinking and Writing,* 4th ed., edited by Gary Colombo, Robert Cullen, and Bonnie Lisle, 612–22. Boston, MA: Bedford/St. Martin's.

Trench, Richard C. 1965. *Proverbs and Their Lessons.* London: Paul Kegan Associates.

Uchendu, Victor C. 1965. *The Igbo of Southeast of Nigeria.* New York: Holt, Rinehart and Winston Press.

United Nations. 1997. *1995 United Nations Demographic Yearbook.* New York: United Nations.

U.S. Bureau of the Census. 1992. *1990 Census of the Population Characteristics, United States.* Washington, D.C.: Government Printing Office.

———. 1993. *The Foreign-Born Population in the U.S. 1990 Census of Population.* Washington, D.C.: Government Printing Office.

U.S. Department of Justice, Immigration and Naturalization Service. 1996. *Statistical Yearbook of the INS, 1994.* Washington, D.C.: Government Printing Office.

———. 1997. *Statistical Yearbook of the INS, 1952–1997.* Washington, D.C.: Government Printing Office.

Wallace, T. 1980. "Agricultural Projects and Land in Northern Nigeria." *Review of African Political Economy* 17: 59–70.

Westernmann, D. 1929. "The Linguistic Situation and Vernacular Literature in British West Africa." *Africa* 2 (4): 337–43.

Willie, Charles V. 1981. *A New Look at Black Families,* 2nd ed. New York: General Hall Printing Co.

Wiseman, John A. 1990. *Democracy in Black Africa and Revival.* New York: Paragon House.

Index

About the Author

KALU OGBAA is Professor of English and Africana Studies at Southern Connecticut State University. He is the author of *Understanding Things Fall Apart: A Student Casebook to Issues, Source, and Historical Documents* (Greenwood, 1999), and *A Century of Nigerian Literature: A Select Bibliography* (2002).